The Tramway Revolution in France 1985-2
"Thirty Glorious Years"
Volume 2: Paris and Île de France

Brian Patton

ISBN 978-0-9564288-8-2

First published in Scotland in 2015 by Brian Patton

Printed and bound by
Martins the Printers Limited
Seaview Works, Spittal
Berwick-upon-Tweed, TD15 1RS
www.martins-the-printers.com

Set in 8.7/10.5 Today
Design by www.simprimstudio.com

In 2009 the Région of Île de France was waging a forceful campaign to draw the attention of the public to its transport projects and these two posters highlighted new tram lines. The dates for their completion proved to be a trifle ambitious.

FRONT COVER

A. "The very model of a modern light rail system." Bound for Porte de Versailles on line T2, No.428 approaches les Coteaux at speed on 22 March 2015.

B. At Noisy-le-Sec on 4 June 2005, no.102 has just left the terminus of line T1 and crosses the bridge spanning the maze of railway tracks to the east of the SNCF station.

BACK COVER

A. On line T4, tram-train no.01 calls at Pavillons-sous-Bois on 4 June 2005.

B. No.62 awaits departure from Robert Wagner, the temporary terminus of line T6, on 22 March 2015.

INTRODUCTION

Many cities have become closely associated with their tramways. Lisbon has its electricòs, Berlin its Trams (never Strassenbahnen!), Oslo its Trikken and Glasgow once had its "caurs" (cars). Citizens and visitors alike have taken these trams to their hearts and in the case of the last-named, looked on them with such affection that almost half the population was prepared to stand in a tropical downpour for an hour to see the last cars pass on their way to the scrapyard. Paris has never been in this category and, given the size of its former network and the increasing spread of its excellent present system, this is surprising.

As far as the former system is concerned, one reason may be that large-scale electrification came late to Paris and was only just completed as the first troops went off to a war which would see France, although technically a victor, bled of much of its best manpower, mired in economic problems and very eager to embrace the demands of the motor lobby of the 1920s. A second and perhaps more important reason could be that, early in the 20th century, the Métro filled the gap created by the heterogeneous character of the tramways in the decade after its first line was opened. With its closely-spaced and easily accessible stations, it was much better placed to compete with the trams than were the tube lines in London or the U-Bahn in Berlin and Parisians flocked to it in their hundreds of thousands. There were some signs that the network of modern tramways which was emerging in the years 1911-1914 would at least slow down the growth in traffic on the underground system and it is interesting – though not especially useful - to speculate how the city's transport might have evolved had war not broken out when it did.

It is more difficult to explain why many people, both Parisians and visitors, seem to be equally indifferent to the very fine modern system which has grown up since 1992, to the extent that many of the latter react with surprise when told that there are modern trams running in Paris and that the city is steadily moving up to join the ranks of world leaders in this field, cities such as Melbourne, Sankt Peterburg and Wien/Vienna. The explanation probably lies in the disjointed nature of the Paris tram system, which has not, as yet, coalesced into a network, and the absence of any lines in the central area. The tourist approaching Paris may catch a glimpse of a green and white tram as the Eurostar dashes through Saint-Denis and the visitor on business at la Défense may just see one disappearing into a tunnel but both will probably look in vain for another while they are in the city. The Paris Métro has always been worked, and worked most successfully, as a system with entirely separate lines and it would seem that the developing tramway system is following the same pattern.

Despite what has been said above, the tram system of Paris has developed steadily in the past quarter-century and it is certainly time to put on record what has been achieved. In fact, so much has happened since the first tram ran on line T1 that only a separate book on the city could do any justice to its creation. It is particularly striking that all those concerned with the planning, construction and operation of new tram lines have wisely avoided a "one size fits all" approach and the tram has thus been able to demonstrate its efficiency in a variety of forms and situations. One line may link different suburbs and obviate the need to go into the centre to reach one from another. Another may be a feeder to the Métro. Yet another fills a gap in the suburban rail network much more effectively than the railway ever did and will soon extend its reach to help rebuild a suburb which has had considerable economic and social problems in the last few decades. Ring lineT3 at last puts right the effect of a bad decision in 1934, when the Petite Ceinture railway was replaced by a bus service. All this has been achieved in conjunction with far-sighted and equally far-reaching schemes of urban improvement, coupled in most cases with a careful restraint of the motor vehicle. The result is helping France to meet its commitments concerning climate change. The trams themselves are specific to their own line and each design has been carefully chosen to fit that line's individual needs. All are excellent examples of their type. The TFS2 trams of lineT1 are still quiet and smooth-riding after 24 years of very hard work and the only criticism that can be made of them is that their design does not allow them to expand to cope with the growth in passenger numbers.

It has been fascinating and inspiring to watch this system develop since 1992 and I hope that something of this will be conveyed to readers by the text and illustrations. The book is intended not simply as an account of the present-day tramways but also as an indication of all the work that has gone into their creation. I appreciate that holes in the ground are not in themselves particularly interesting, but if there had not been holes in the ground, trams would not now be running on the new lines. All but a few photographs are by me or from my collection and only those by others are credited. In the few cases where street or station names have been changed over the years, the present name is given in brackets. A summary of references is given after each chapter and a complete bibliography can be found at the end of the book.

Unless otherwise credited, illustrations are by the author or from the author's collection.

Once again I have to thank M Yves Allain of Clermont-Ferrand who with pleasure undertook the major task of reading the ms, not only to check the contents but also to advise on points of information which would not be clear to someone who is not a citizen of France. Without his contribution the book would not have been complete and I am most grateful to him. I have also to thank Jim Schantz of Boston for his help with the illustrations.

Brian Patton
Foulden, Berwickshire, Scotland
4 November 2015

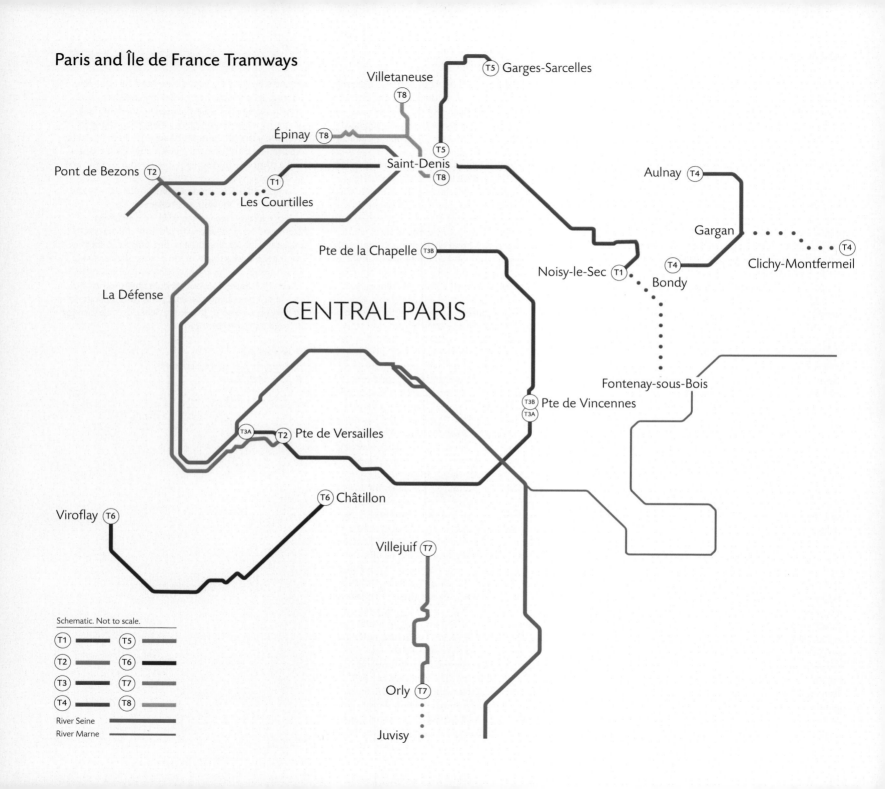

Paris and Île de France Tramways

Villetaneuse (T8)

(T5) Garges-Sarcelles

Épinay (T8)

Saint-Denis

(T5)

(T8)

Aulnay (T4)

Pont de Bezons (T2)

(T1)

Les Courtilles

Gargan

La Défense

Pte de la Chapelle (T3B)

Noisy-le-Sec (T1)

Bondy (T4)

Clichy-Montfermeil (T4)

CENTRAL PARIS

Fontenay-sous-Bois

(T3B)
(T3A) Pte de Vincennes

(T3A) (T2) Pte de Versailles

(T6) Châtillon

Viroflay (T6)

Villejuif (T7)

Schematic. Not to scale.

(T1) —— (T5) ——
(T2) —— (T6) ——
(T3) —— (T7) ——
(T4) —— (T8) ——

River Seine ——
River Marne ——

Orly (T7)

Juvisy

Contents

Chapter 1
The Historical Background

The city of Paris itself is smaller than many visitors expect, with to-day a population of just over 2.2 million. Immediately before the first French revolution, its area consisted, in broad terms, of the area enclosed by lines 2 and 6 of the Métro and around this, in 1788, there was erected a wall, pierced by many gates. The purpose of this wall was financial, rather than defensive, since the government of Louis XVI was by that date very short of money. To take goods into Paris, citizens had to pay a tax known as the "octroi", this being collected by agents known as the "Fermiers généraux" (Tax farmers). The wall was and sometimes is still referred to as "L'enceinte (enclosure) des fermiers généraux". Of course the octroi did not stave off the revolution and one result of it was the division, in October 1795, of the area within the wall into twelve arrondissements (districts), while the city was given an elected mayor and its own council. The former post did not last for long, elected mayors not being to the taste of Napoléon I, but the council did survive. Paris was not to have a mayor again until 1977, when Jacques Chirac became the first to assume that post in modern times.

During the reign of Louis-Philippe (1830-1848) the city received a defensive fortification, often known as "L'enceinte de Thiers" from the First Minister who arranged its construction. It was 10m high and encircled Paris at what was then its outer limits. This wall was pierced by 49 gates, generally about 520m apart, as well as openings for railways and canals. Behind it ran a continuous road 7.5m wide, linking all the gates. Under Napoléon III (1852-1870), this narrow road became the boulevard des Maréchaux, its various sections being given the names of marshals of the First or Second Empires. It was planted with a double row of trees. With the enthusiastic support of the Emperor and under the direction of G-E Haussmann, a great deal of urban renewal was undertaken in central Paris at this time, much being at the expense of the poorer citizens who could not afford the rents demanded for the fine new apartments and who migrated in droves to the area between the two walls, in which fourteen settlements developed in a somewhat chaotic manner. In 1859, Empress Eugénie, as Regent, signed into law a decree

dividing these into eight new arrondissements, thus doubling the size of the city and bringing some order into the chaos. This change came into effect on 1 January 1860, and the gates in the outer wall became the points at which the octroi was collected. Both walls were demolished in the years 1921-25 and much of the space occupied by the second was used to build housing, to be let at moderate rents. The areas concerned were added to these arrondissements. During the Vichy regime, Marshall Pétain allocated the remaining area to Paris and proposed to use it after the war for a green boulevard, but for obvious reasons this plan was dropped in 1944. Otherwise the area of Paris has not changed since 1860. However, although almost a century has elapsed since the outer wall was demolished, the entire area of the city is still often referred to as "Paris intra muros" (Paris within the walls).

Until 1963, Paris was completely surrounded by the Département of la Seine, whose Prefect had considerable authority over the city, as did the Prefect of Police, who had overall responsibility for a range of issues of security, some of which involved transport. Between 1860 and 1914, the rural areas adjacent to Paris gradually developed into suburbs of the city such as Montrouge and Aubervilliers and by the latter year these suburbs accounted for almost 30% of the population of the metropolitan area. The process continued with much greater force after 1918 and by 1926 some had developed into large towns in their own right. Saint-Denis had a population of almost 80,000 in 1926 and Boulogne and Levallois were not far behind. By 1939 the suburbs had a population of two million, while the city had 2.8 million. The resulting daily commuting increased in step with these developments, with a particularly steep increase between 1924 and 1931. This area is often referred to as "la banlieue de la petite couronne", a title which in English can only be rendered, much less poetically, as the inner suburbs. After 1945 the main area of development was that beyond these suburbs, in what is correspondingly known as "la grande couronne" or outer suburbs. While these new suburbs were somewhat chaotically growing, the city itself began to lose population and the total sank to two million, from which it has since slightly recovered to about 2.2

million. This figure has to be seen against a total of 11.26 million for the Région of Île-de-France.

There was little attempt to regulate the development of the entire region in the inter-war years, during which the only competition to public transport was the bicycle. The only measure published was the Projet d'aménagement de la région Parisienne de 1934, generally known as the Plan Proust after its author, Henri Proust. Unfortunately it was not finally adopted until 1941 and as the Vichy government tended to favour the provinces rather than the capital, very little of it resulted in any action. After 1945 the growth of the suburbs resumed its course, soon to be accompanied by a vast increase in the number of private cars and commercial vehicles in the region. From totals of 1.35 million and 600,000 in 1950, these had increased to 12.28 million and 2.11 million twenty years later.[1]

As the administrative structure of local government no longer fitted the actual situation, a District of the Paris region was created in 1961, though as its powers were limited, it achieved little. Two years later the Départements of la Seine (75) and la Seine et Oise (78) were divided between two new départements, Seine-Saint-Denis (93, north and north-east) and Hauts-de-Seine (92, west), and the existing Département of Val-de-Marne (94, south-east and south). These now make up the Petite Couronne. Further out, four other départements were created – Seine et Marne (77, east), Essonne (91, south), Yvelines (78, west) and Val d'Oise (95, north) and these form the Grande Couronne. The individual communes in the areas of these authorities have certain powers relating to transport planning and mayors have not been shy of exercising these. In 1976 the District, with much enlarged powers, became the Région of Île-de-France, which has the same powers as the other regions created in 1972. Its inhabitants are often referred to as Franciliens.

In the years after 1945, the population of the metropolitan area increased rapidly. This increase was not distributed evenly over the whole of Île-de-France but was particularly marked in the outer suburbs. This trend has continued to the present day, although between 1999 and 2008, the increase was

---

1 P Merlin, Transports et Urbanisme en Île-de-France.

greatest in the inner suburbs. Contemporaneously with this growth, the various governments developed the network of motorways, particularly in the 1970s and these had an effect on suburban transport. Many other roads followed, all feeding into the capital at various points and in some cases also linking with the boulevard périphérique. As in other countries, this new system of roads opened up possibilities for commuting, the lack of effective public transport links between the outer suburbs having tended to discourage this. In 1991 there were 296 private vehicles (mainly cars) per 1,000 inhabitants within Paris and that number had increased by only 24% since 1962, just over half of all households still not having private transport. By 2010 this figure had increased to 55%. By contrast, there were 442.5 per 1,000 inhabitants in the outer suburbs and the increase since 1962 had been of the order of 55%. Journeys between different suburbs were by 1991 most often made by car (80%) while public transport accounted for only 15.9% and cycles only 0.3%. These trends were especially marked in the peak hours. In the evening peak in 1991-92, the private car was used only for 16.5% of journeys within Paris but for 68.7% of journeys between suburbs. In the inner suburbs, the average number of cars per household was now 0.92 while in the outer suburbs it was 1.35, 40% of households now having two cars.[2]

It should be noted that, unlike London, Paris has not at any time been surrounded by settlements, such as Kingston or Ilford, towns in their own right which in due course would grow inwards to meet an expanding centre. There was only the royal town of Versailles and the much smaller centres of Saint-Denis to the north and Saint-Germain to the west. Otherwise Paris stood in splendid isolation.

Until the appearance in 1965 of the first Schéma directeur d'aménagement et d'urbanisme de la Région de Paris (Guidelines for the urban development of the Paris region), there was little effective overall planning and no attempt to link housing and commercial development with transport. This document was prepared from 1961 to 1964 by M Paul Delouvrier, a high-ranking civil servant attached to the District of the Paris region, and it was intended that it should "constituer un outil de recherche et étude, convenablement pourvu d'hommes et de moyens matériels" (act as a tool for research and study, suitably provided with staff

and equipment). It was certainly an advance on what had gone before, although, largely at the behest of President de Gaulle, it was limited in parts to little more than a list of polite exhortations. It was slightly revised in 1969 and again in 1976, when it became much more directive. Adoption of the Schéma led to the building of five new towns, such as Evry, Cergy-Pontoise and Saint-Quentin-en-Yvelines, in the Grande Couronne, the construction of the boulevard périphérique, completed in 1973 (much of it on the land originally set aside by Marshall Pétain to be used as green spaces after the war) and the first line (A) of the RER. However, it did little for other public transport in the area. Once adopted, the Schéma has legal force to allow its recommendations to be translated into practice. Meanwhile central government was beginning to take more notice of the Région and of local transport and on 24 July 1989 Michel Rocard (PS), at that date First Minister, outlined the plans for the next 25 years which would keep the Région, and so the nation, at the forefront of world metropolitan areas, these plans to form part of a new Schéma directeur, consultation on which was launched in 1990. The Council of the Région, under its President M P-C Krieg was also considering its recommendations, with the aim of avoiding the creation of "une vaste mégapole inhumaine" (a great megalopolis, not on a human scale) and, for the first time in these debates, mentioning the environment. The final document was adopted in 1994 and as its scope had been enlarged to include the entire area of Île-de-France its title was changed accordingly.

One of the proposals it contained was the creation of Orbitale – Organisation du Bassin Intérieur en Transport Automatique liberé des Encombrements (Serving the inner suburbs by a system of automatic transport on its own right-of-way). This would be a series of lines around the circumference of the city, a length of 170km, to be worked (despite the "automatic") in some sections by trams and in others by light automatic metros. Tram line T1, already in service, and the proposed line T2, would be incorporated into this system, with some extensions of the former. To serve the areas lying further out from the centre, there were proposals for a new system of mainline ring railways, using SNCF tracks and named Lutèce – Liaison à utilisation tangentielle en Couronne Extérieure (Tangential links in the outer suburbs). Lutèce is also the Roman name of Paris. Concrete plans for other surface transport were for

the first time outlined, these including the orbital lines mentioned above, as well as radial lines. The network of heavy rail lines was to be complemented by one of lines "en site propre" (on their own right-of-way) and among others were lines to serve Villetanneuse University from Saint-Denis, Garges-Sarcelles from Saint-Denis, and Orly and Juvisy from Villejuif. These would ultimately become tram lines T8, T5 and T7. The lines which would become T4, T6 and the branch of line T8 to Épinay were added at a later date.

After President Sarkozy assumed office in 2007, there were developed grandiose plans for what he referred to as "le Grand Paris", some of which revived the Orbitale proposals but with full-size automatic métros whizzing between great centres of technology to be located in what are at present greenfield sites, and which were what German commentators politely called "überdimensionierte" (on too grand a scale). In view of the new proposals and the many legal changes made after 1994, a new version of the Schéma directeur was brought out in 2008. The original plans caused conflict between the President, his First Minister François Fillon and the Région, under the presidency of M Jean-Paul Huchon, who looked for something much more attuned to the needs of local people. After a good deal of noisy and sometimes acrimonious discussion, a reasonable compromise was reached on 26 January 2011 and this was later adopted after M Hollande assumed the presidency and M Jean-Marc Ayrault, Mayor of Nantes, became First Minister. A protocol was signed on 19 July 2013 between central government and the Région governing spending on transport between 2013 and 2017. In conjunction with these plans, it is likely that in 2017 a new authority should come into being, covering almost exactly the city and the area of the former Département de la Seine. How this will co-exist with the Région or the outer Départements is not at present clear and the results of the forthcoming regional elections in December 2015 may change these plans. Not everyone is convinced of the need for circumferential Métro lines and many think that the money would be better spent on upgrading the existing networks.

As far as tramways are concerned, the main proposals to emerge from the discussions were a revival of part of the Lutèce proposals, but using tram-trains, running on their own tracks rather than sharing SNCF tracks. The lines are:-

2 Enquête globale des transports, 2014.

❏ North-east from Sartrouville to Noisy-le-Sec, with possible later extensions to Sucy-Bonneuil and Massy-Palaiseau.
❏ West, from Saint-Cyr to Cergy-Pontoise.
❏ South-east, from Versailles Chantiers to Corby-Essonnes via Massy-Palaiseau and Évry.

The findings of the Enquête globale des Transports 2010 have suggested that the use of public transport in Île-de-France is at last increasing. It also showed that the growth in the use of the car, at 5% per annum in the 1980s, had ceased. Between 2001 and 2010, the daily use of public transport, in terms of passenger journeys, increased by 21% to 8.3 million, against an increase in car use of only 0.06%. The most startling change was that 33% of this increase was in off-peak travel during the day. Within Paris itself, car use was down by 35%. Not only public transport saw an increase – cycling was the preferred mode for 650,000 people per day, 4.3% of the total – and walking had also increased. The PDU approved in December 2014, covering the years 2020-2030, proposed a further increase of 20% in the use of public transport. and 10% in "les modes actifs" (walking and cycling) with a decrease of 2% each in the case of cars and motor cycles.

The changes already noted will have been brought about by many social and economic factors but the improvements made to public transport, including the opening of the new tram lines, must have played a part. Not everything envisaged in the plans adopted in 1994 has as yet come to pass but for the tram in and around Paris, these were crucial and much has been achieved.

Before reviewing the present system, the history of the tramways in the area has to be considered. What follows is a very brief summary of a complex story. To put this into perspective, it should perhaps be mentioned that the definitive history of the tram in Paris, by M Jean Robert, is a weighty volume of 575 pages.

Chapter 2
The Development of Public Transport

The political structure of local government has had a profound effect on public transport in and around Paris. The first buses ran in the city in 1828 and in 1855 the various competing companies which had entered the field were, on the order of J-M Piétri, the Prefect of Police, with the agreement of Haussmann and the Emperor, amalgamated into the Compagnie Générale des Omnibus (CGO). In that year the tram arrived in the city, when a French engineer, François-Alphonse Loubat, who had worked on tramways in the USA, received permission to open a line, to be worked by horse trams, between place de l'Alma and the rond-point de Boulogne and this was opened in September 1855. Standard gauge was used. As the line did not produce the expected profits, Loubat was happy to sell it to the CGO on 1 July 1857, by which date it had been extended inwards to place de la Concorde. It was later extended outwards to Versailles and inwards to Louvre (using road-rail cars), but no more lines were opened until after the Franco-Prussian war of 1870-71.

To serve the working-class suburbs that were developing in the new arrondissements, especially in the north-east of the city, the CGO on 18 June 1860 obtained a new concession from the City, whose politicians were concerned that there should be adequate omnibus services to these areas. In return for an agreement to provide such services, which were unlikely to be profitable in the short term, the CGO was granted a monopoly of road passenger transport within the entire area of Paris, in a concession which was to run until 31 May 1910.

As yet the mainline railways played a very small part in the internal transport of the city. At week-ends there was a good deal of pleasure traffic to areas such as Saint-Germain, but regular commuting to work by train was virtually unknown. The only exceptions to this were a short line between Saint-Lazare and Auteuil, opened in 1855, and the Petite Ceinture line, which was completed as a circle in 1867, incorporating part of the former line in its course. At the insistence of the government, a passenger service had been instituted on the Petite Ceinture from July 1862 and gradually this service became very popular, carrying 39 million passengers in 1900, though this figure was inflated by exhibition traffic and 31 million

was probably a normal annual average. For most of its course, the line followed the outer wall around the city.

By the time matters had returned to near-normal after the war of 1870-71, the demand for the installation of tram services had grown and in 1872 the Prefect of the Seine set up a commission to study and report on the creation of "Un réseau des voies ferrées desservies par des chevaux, dans Paris et sa banlieue". (A network of [street] railways, served by horse drawn traffic, in Paris and its suburbs.) The commission worked with commendable speed and presented its favourable report in the summer of 1873. The decree authorising its proposals was signed by President Mac Mahon on 9 August 1873, conceding to the Département a network of ten radial lines and one circular line. The latter was awarded to the CGO, along with the inner sections of the radial lines. It did not come into operation as a circle and was divided into five sections as part of the radial lines. The portions of these that lay outwith the city were given to two new companies, the Tramways Nord and the Tramways Sud (the latter had British capital) and in practice these also worked the inner portions of their lines, infringing the monopoly of the CGO within Paris. The concession was also to run until 31 May 1910. As the CGO dealt with the City, the new companies with the Département and the syndicate of the Petite Ceinture with central government, the new structure was a recipe for confusion.

The various tram lines were opened between 1874 and 1878 and by the latter year 11 lines, including Loubat's line, were run by the CGO in Paris (lettered TA to TK). There were 20 in the suburbs, nine run by the Tramways Nord (A and AB to TH) and eleven by the Tramways Sud (1-11). The approach of the international exhibition of 1878 had given the impetus for this rapid development and on 21 August 1877 the CGO was awarded a concession for six new lines. After 1879 stagnation set in, largely because the two new companies, whose fares were tied to those of the CGO, operated at a loss. In 1884 both were declared bankrupt, proposals for a merger with the CGO having been turned down by the authorities. In 1888 their lines passed to two new companies, the Cie des Tramways de Paris et du Département de la Seine

(TPDS) in the north and the Cie Générale Parisienne de Tramways (CGPT) in the south. In 1887 two other companies entered the tramway field. The Cie des Chemins de fer Nogentais (CFN) began to operate lines in the affluent eastern suburbs, where there was also a good deal of pleasure traffic at week-ends. This company was set up by Louis Mékarski, as a means of demonstrating his system of compressed air traction in the Paris area and the Nogentais proved to be successful and profitable. Double-deck cars, with similar trailers, were used. Its nine lines, of 52km length, were electrified in 1900, using overhead current collection. There was also a funeral tram, in use at Vincennes. The other company operated a service of steam trams between Paris and Saint-Germain. In 1911 its lines were converted to electric operation.

In 1881 an Electricity Exhibition was held in the Palais de l'Industrie[1] and naturally Siemens of Berlin was an exhibitor. To link the site with the place de la Concorde, that company built what was only its third tramway, a line of 493m length. Unlike the practice in Berlin, the running rails could not be used to supply live current or as a return, "due to the state of the roads", and so this line became the first anywhere to use an overhead form of current collection. This took the form of two bronze, slotted tubes suspended about 5m above rail level. One was positive and one negative and a collector slid in each, which passed current to and from the motors by a flexible cable linked to a pole on the upper deck. The tram used was a double-ended double-decker of the Tramways Nord. Service began on 10 August 1881 and continued satisfactorily until the end of the exhibition. Paris thus became the first city to have an electric tramway with overhead current collection. However, if Werner von Siemens was hoping that this temporary display might lead to the installation of a permanent line, he was to be sadly disappointed and Paris was to lag behind most other European capitals (except Edinburgh) in the introduction of electric trams using overhead wires.

Cable traction came to Paris on 25 August 1891 in the form of a metre gauge line, 2km long, from place de la République up to the hilly area of Belleville. Despite protests by the CGO, which feared an infringement of its monopoly, it was operated for the City by the Cie du Tramway Funiculaire de Belleville and, possibly because of its title, it was often referred to as a funicular, although it was in fact a cable tramway, such as operated in south London and Edinburgh. The fare was 10c up and 5c down. Passenger numbers grew, as the line served a densely-populated area which had no other effective form of public transport and 3,398,000 passengers were carried in 1892. There were 21 trams, each with a capacity of 22 passengers. Due to the restricted width of the street, it could only be a single line with passing loops and lack of capacity soon became a major problem which was finally solved by running the cars in coupled pairs, accommodating 57 passengers. There were occasional accidents, but none was serious, although that which occurred in June 1914, when the cable broke and a car ran away, was certainly spectacular. The tramway was profitable and popular and someone once wrote a song about it, ("Pour monter à Belleville miron ton ton mirontaine y avait un p'tit tramway"), set to the tune of "Malbrook s'en va t'en guerre"[2]. The line was replaced by a bus service in 1924. Its main claim to later fame is that the engineer in charge of its construction was Fulgence Bienvenüe, who some years later would be responsible for the building of the Métro.

The international exhibition of 1889 once again showed up the inadequacy of the public transport network and the need to expand the tramways. In that year, the CGO carried almost 147 million passengers (buses and trams) and the other companies carried 64 million[3]. As the City and the CGO were now on very bad terms and the City, the mainline railways and the Département were quarrelling about the construction of an underground railway, central government stepped in and, in 1890, issued new concessions, with the same expiry date, to the CGO, the TPDS and the CGPT for a total of nine new lines and one extension. While these new lines offered a much-needed boost to the system, they did nothing to solve the basic problems arising from the competition between the three main companies.

During this period, the question of electrification began to arise, but with concessions of only a limited duration, it was unlikely that any of the companies would want to spend a great deal on their network. The Tramways Nord had in fact experimented with an accumulator car from September 1888 to January 1889; it ran on line C from Levallois in the north-west to Madeleine and appeared to be satisfactory, with the result that the successor company, the TPDS, was authorised to use this form of traction on its line to Saint-Denis. Line E, Saint-Denis – Madeleine was converted to accumulator cars in April 1892. The journey time to Saint-Denis was reduced to 55 minutes, against 90 with horse cars, but the batteries gave off fumes and in winter, when the windows were closed, the atmosphere in the lower saloon became unbearable. No more conversions took place at that time.

A further operator to use compressed air was the Compagnie des Tramways de Saint-Maur, in the south-eastern suburbs, whose first line opened on 1 March 1894. The CGO, which still showed no enthusiasm for electrification, was also considering compressed air as the motive power for a new line, TAD, Saint-Augustin – Cours de Vincennes. Its length was 9.1km and the line traversed some steep gradients on its eastern part, notably around Belleville. It was rather long and certainly had too many gradients to be worked by horses and it was therefore decided to equip it for compressed air working. The line was quickly constructed and double-deck cars began to operate over its eastern part on 7 August 1894. These proved to be so successful that they were extended to the entire line and from May 1895 pulled trailer cars. Several other lines were converted in 1895/6. On these, up to three trailer cars were pulled by a locomotive.

Yet another form of traction appeared on 1 June 1896 when a line was opened by the Cie du Tramway de Paris à Romainville (in the north-east), which broadly followed the course of the present Métro line 11, with an extension at its outer end. The novelty of this electric line was that it used a system of current collection by studs placed in the roadway between the running rails. There were problems, as the studs sometimes did not respond to the collector under the car when it passed over and so caused it to stop, while in other cases studs remained live after a car had passed, with predictable consequences to horses and pedestrians, while a heavy downpour often produced quite spectacular short-circuits, with accompanying fireworks. In spite of these troubles, the line was successful, with three million passengers in 1896, and the company was even able to spare enough electricity to light the avenue de la République and the avenue

---

1 On the line of the present avenue Alexandre III. It was demolished in 1898/9 to make way for the Grand Palais.

2 A folk song popular in France in the 18th and 19th centuries, purporting to report the death of the Duke of Marlborough after the Battle of Malplaquet in 1709. In fact he survived until 1722.

3 Merlin, op.cit.

Gambetta. However, no other company adopted the stud contact system. The line later became part of the system of the Cie des Tramways de l'Est Parisien and the studs were abandoned in 1910.

A steam tram had been demonstrated in Paris as early as 1875, when on 8 November the English entrepreneur G P Harding showed an example to an assembled group of notables, including President Mac Mahon. On the strength of a trial between Porte de Châtillon and Saint-Germain-des-Prés, Harding was granted permission to run the line of the Tramways Sud between Gare Montparnasse and place Valhubert (near the Gare d'Austerlitz) with steam power and this service, the first use of a steam tram in urban service in Europe, began on 9 August 1876. The need to have two men on each locomotive led to a reversion to horse power in February 1878. Other companies made brief but unsuccessful trials. It was not until 1895, when the TPDS began an experiment with steam trams on line D, Gennevilliers – Madeleine, that the steam tram really arrived in Paris. This line was worked by double-deck cars using the Purrey system of steam traction and another line followed in the next year. The company then decided to convert the entire system (save one short branch line in Saint-Ouen) to electric traction. This was accomplished by 1899, the steam-worked lines also being converted. As it was not permitted to use overhead current collection within Paris, the cars used accumulators within the city and overhead line collection outwith its limits. The batteries were recharged as the tram progressed and this avoided the time-consuming matter of changing these while the car was in service. In 1900 the TPDS operated trams on 22 lines with a total route length of 130km.

The CGPT meanwhile had realised that it could not continue for much longer with its very well-run horse-powered system, but it had no interest in electrifying its lines with accumulator trams. In 1896 therefore it began talks with the City to allow it to use overhead wires within Paris, these to be confined to the main arteries and trams to be worked across squares and other places of architectural merit on the conduit system. Somewhat grudgingly, and only after some delay, the municipality gave its assent "à titre d'essai" (on a trial basis) to the conversion of the line along the avenue Daumesnil, adding as a condition that the Company should provide electric lighting, with arc lamps, on that important artery. Both conversions were duly executed and electric trams began running

on 9 November 1898. The new service (and the lamps) proved very popular and the success of this conversion clearly pointed the way ahead. In 1900 the CGPT had 13 lines with a route length of 124km.

A ministerial decree of 16 February 1900 imposed various conditions on the operators of tramways within Paris. The maximum speed was to be 25km/hr, cars were to be heated and lit and two classes were to be carried, in the proportion of one third first class to two thirds second. The overhead trolley was not to be used within Paris. The working day of crews was reduced.

The CGO, now operating 33 lines (260km), seemed to be content to rest on its laurels and allow the other operators to experiment. It was profitable and, as its concession would expire in 1910, managers and shareholders saw no point in spending vast sums on electrifying its tramways. But with the approach of another international exhibition (1900), whose main theme was to be "La Fée Électricité" (The Magic of Electricity), its system would appear to be old-fashioned and Paris would be considered backward in comparison with cities such as Glasgow, which was not even a national capital and where full-scale conversion to electric traction (with overhead wires) was progressing smoothly and rapidly, together with preparations for an international exhibition, to be held in 1901. The other companies in the Paris area were improving their systems and new operators were entering the field. It therefore introduced four new services, all operated by horse trams, to serve the exhibition and embarked on a hurried programme of conversion of its lines variously to steam (one line), compressed air (five) and accumulator propulsion, mainly using double-deck cars.[4] It was keeping its options open.

Trams were among the large exhibits displayed at the exhibition, some in the Civil Engineering Pavilion at Champ de Mars and some in the annexe at Vincennes, to serve which the Nogentais company built a special line. There were in total 25, of which 17 were French. The CGO displayed four, all fitted with its standard double-deck body. These were compressed-air car no.128, Purrey steam car no.722, Serpollet steam car no.801 and accumulator car no.586. But, reading in the book Merveilles de l'Exposition "De fée qu'elle était, l'électricité est devenue une souveraine toute puissante, investie par le génie humain d'un pouvoir infini" (magic though it was, electricity has

become an all-conquering sovereign, endowed by human ingenuity with infinite power), visitors could be forgiven if they wondered why the CGO was bothering with this variety of alternative forms of propulsion for its trams. All were reported to be slow and noisy.

Moreover, the conflict between the City and the Département having at last been settled, construction of the Métro by the former began in the autumn of 1898, with a view to opening the first line in 1900, in time to serve the exhibition and, slightly late, this was achieved on 19 July of that year. The system was built by the City but run by a private company, the Compagnie du Chemin de fer Métropolitain de Paris (CMP). With its closely-spaced stations – the average distance between these on its early lines was only 440m – and the easy access to these stations, which were mostly only just below street level, it was obvious that the new system would be a strong competitor for traffic within Paris and that the operator who was likely to suffer most would be the CGO. As the Métro did not then run beyond the city boundary, the tram lines that served the suburbs retained a competitive advantage on through services, although there was some interchange with the new system at the various gates, such as Porte de Vincennes. The use of all public transport was growing and none of the main companies suffered a loss of traffic in the first decade of the 20th century.

Other operators of tramways in the Paris area, as of 31 May 1910, were:

1. The Compagnie des Tramways de l'Est Parisien, operating six lines in the east. In 1921 298 motor cars and 108 trailers passed to the STCRP.
2. The Compagnie des Tramways Mécaniques des Environs de Paris, operating six lines (35km), entirely outwith the city, in the western and north-western suburbs. It passed to the TPDS in 1910.
3. Compagnie Électrique des Tramways de la Rive Gauche, operating two lines (35km) from Porte de Vincennes. (63 motor cars and 24 trailers in 1921).
4. The Compagnie du Chemin de fer du Bois de Boulogne, operating in the south-western suburbs. It had 22 motor cars and 43 trailers in 1921.
5. The Compagnie des Tramways Nord-Parisien, with one line from the city to Saint-Denis and Épinay. It became part of the TPDS system in 1910.
6. The Société du Chemin de fer sur Route de Paris à Arpajon, operating a long radial line through and beyond the southern suburbs. It used steam

4 Historail, July 2014

locomotives and compressed air and later electric trams on the inner section. In 1921 it had 50 electric motors and 68 trailers in its fleet.

7. The Compagnie des Tramways de l'Ouest Parisien, operating some short lines in the western suburbs. (50 motors and 12 trailers in 1921.)

The early tramways certainly brought some colour to the streets of the capital. The CGO used colour to differentiate forms of motive power. Compressed air cars were painted dark green, accumulator cars were dark red with a black dash and steam cars were even sub-divided by type, Purrey cars being chocolate and Serpollet cars yellow. The TPDS used green, except for one class (C), which was yellow and the TPDS trams were yellow, latterly with black ends. Trams of the EP, CFBB, Nogentais and TMEP all used yellow.

With the ending of the various concessions in 1910, the way was at last clear for a degree of co-ordination of road transport in Paris and the surrounding area and, by a ministerial decree of 19 August, new concessions were granted, that to the CGO being conditional on its electrifying all its lines on the overhead or (in the city centre) conduit system. Given that the CGO alone operated 30 lines, only one of which used overhead current collection, this was achieved remarkably quickly, as was the conversion of the bus services to motor vehicles. The first tram line to be converted was line TE, Nation – la Villette, which became line 7 on 18 June 1912. The last line with horse cars, line TV Pantin - Opéra was converted on 20 April 1913 and the last mechanically-powered trams ran between June and August 1914. The last was on line TAE from Madeleine to Boulogne, which changed from compressed air to electric working, as part of line 16, on 2 August 1914, by which date France was at war. The fleet now consisted of 586 new motor cars and 325 trailers. All depots and the central workshops at Championnet had been adapted and modernised. Meanwhile the road service was being motorised and the last horse bus ran in 1913. The entire conversion was a marvellous achievement and passenger numbers increased considerably as the conversion progressed. It was also noticeable that the rate of growth in passenger numbers on the Métro slowed in 1912 and became negative in 1913 and the first part of 1914. The other companies carried out similar programmes and the nine companies now operated a network of 923km. The way ahead seemed to be very promising

for the tramways of Paris, despite the continuing development of the Métro.

Unfortunately the war and associated post-war economic and social problems, with wage and price inflation, completely upset the financial basis on which the concessions were based. By 1920 fares had been increased by 75%, despite which all companies made a loss. The Département had to step in and assume control of all forms of surface transport, setting up the Société des Transports en Commun de la Région Parisienne (STCRP), which began operation on 1 January 1921. All the main companies were amalgamated on that date and three minor operators joined by 1924, when unified control was at last achieved. As the head of the new organisation was M André Mariage, previously manager of the CGO, the practices of the latter largely continued with the new arrangement. The Métro remained the responsibility of the City and was still run by the CMP. A livery of dark green and ivory was adopted. A consultative committee on public transport in the Paris area was also set up.

There were then 112 lines in operation, over a track length of 960km. Many lines crossed the city boundary and so provided direct services from the suburbs to central Paris. In its early years the new authority, which had inherited 2,300 motor and 930 trailer cars, of more than fifty types, showed considerable enthusiasm for the tram. Workshop facilities were rationalised, much track was relaid, some extensions were opened, a large number of new cars was built and many older vehicles were modernised. In 1925 there were plans for express tramways. The trams carried 734 million passengers in 1929[5]. However, the growth of motor traffic and, perhaps more importantly, the growth of a road lobby soon began to change public and official opinion to one which considered that the trams caused "congestion" and should be eliminated. As trams were legally limited to speeds of 20km/hr within Paris and 30km/hr outwith the city boundary (compared to 45km/hr for buses), there seemed to be a certain amount of justification for this. In some cases, as at place de l'Étoile, where trams were obliged to run contra-flow when new traffic management schemes with one-way streets were introduced, operation became increasingly difficult. In the post-war years, the number of passengers entering the Métro at stations such as Porte de Vincennes and Porte

Maillot grew to the point where these became the busiest stations after some in the central area such as Saint-Lazare. Local politicians began to see the tram as "L'archaïsme grossier, la bétise profonde et la malfaisance certaine" (The crude anachronism, of profound stupidity and certainly harmful). A report by Émile Jayot to the consultative committee in 1928 proposed the extension of the underground system into the suburbs and the Conseil générale de la Seine on 12 July 1928 agreed to a plan for 15 such extensions. The City had already, on 27 December 1927, agreed with this proposal. The dice were being loaded against the tram.

Unlike the schemes of London and West Berlin, the tramways of Paris were closed in a piecemeal fashion which was at times very inconvenient for the travelling public. In 1927 the transport office of the Département of the Seine prepared a plan to eliminate trams within the limits of the wall of the Fermiers Généraux, effectively the inner city, though all lines in the well-to-do areas of Neuilly and the 16th arrondissement had gone by 1930. Tram lines that terminated at places such as place de la République were cut back to the gates of the city and through passengers had to change, this leading to chaotic scenes at peak hours. An example of this was the conversion of the lines from Madeleine to Gennevilliers (39) and Argenteuil (40), which in May 1932 were terminated at Porte de Clichy while a new bus line, confusingly numbered 39/40, took over the inner section. It had been announced that the lines in the suburbs, which involved a good deal of reserved track, would not be converted but in 1932 the Council of the Département agreed to a plan of total abandonment, ostensibly in the interests of other traffic. The authorities may also have wanted to portray Paris as a thoroughly modern metropolis to visitors to the international exhibition of 1937. The outer sections of lines 39 and 40 were converted on 14 April 1936. The programme was virtually completed when the last tram on line 123/124 from Porte de Vincennes to Porte de Saint-Cloud ran into Malakoff depot on 15 March 1937. Only a handful of spectators turned out to witness the event. Due to a disagreement with the local authority about the replacement bus service, suburban line 112 from le Raincy to Montfermeil continued to run until 14 August 1938. It is unlikely that any visitors to the exhibition were aware of its continued existence. The last trams in the Paris area were those of the municipal

---
5 H Bunle in Bulletin de la statistique générale de la France 1932

systems of Versailles and Fontainebleau which continued to run, until 1957 and 1953 respectively.

The STCRP had built 575 new motor trams and 395 trailer cars between 1921 and 1930, as well as modernising over 1,000 of the best cars taken over from the former companies (mainly the CGO), many of which had been built between 1910 and 1914. In addition it had relaid 123km of track, modernised many depots and constructed a completely new depot, at Charlebourg. The abandonment of such a modern system represented a waste of money on a colossal scale and illustrates the power of the road lobby. Many had cause to regret it during the war, when Paris was almost totally bereft of surface transport and only the Métro saved the city from paralysis.

Most lines were converted to motorbuses, although a few were subsequently turned over to trolleybuses. The last of these was abandoned on 1 April 1966 and thereafter the bus reigned supreme in surface transport, although as traffic grew and congestion increased, the network became steadily less efficient and passenger numbers declined.

There were also two events of some significance in 1934. The first extension of the Métro outwith Paris was opened on 3 February 1934, when line 9 was extended to Pont de Sèvres. It was followed by many others, though due to the second world war, some were not opened until after 1945 and two extensions, for lines 4 and 11, have still not been completed. The new lines did not penetrate very far into the suburbs concerned, mostly terminating at the Mairie (mayor's office), which is usually located in the centre of a commune, and through passengers from the outer areas still had to change at some point. The other event was the abandonment of passenger service on the Petite Ceinture railway line in 1934, which now carried only five million passengers per year. It was replaced by a bus service, designated PC.

During the second world war, the Vichy government placed the STCRP under the control of the CMP, although this did not lead to any integration of services. Possibly this was because there were very few bus services to integrate. It was not a satisfactory form of organisation, in that a private company had control over a public body, and, after an intermission from 1945 to 1948 when the Métro was placed under a provisional administration, both organisations were amalgamated into the Régie autonome des Transports Parisiens (RATP) on 1 January 1949. Another body,

the Syndicat des Transports Parisiens (STP) was set up to oversee long-term planning, but for many years this remained a token organisation and it was not until the 1970s that it began to play any meaningful role in transport. It has since been enlarged as the Syndicat des Transports de l'Île de France (STIF) and it is now closely involved not only in planning but also in financing developments. An example of this co-operation is the agreement, settled in January 2011, by which new trams for the extension of line T3 and for new lines T5-T8 were to be financed, to the tune of €378 million, by STIF.

In 2015 the RATP operated a system of eight separate tram lines, with a total route length of 104.4 km. Planned extensions to these lines will add another 29.8km in the next few years and further new tram lines and tram-train services will follow after 2018. Paris will then have the fifth-largest tramway system in the world though, due to the separation of the various lines, this status may not be realised by visitors to the city. Each line is worked entirely on its own and there is no through running between different lines and indeed at present no track connexions.

The wheel has come full circle and Paris and its suburbs are once again served by trams. It is now time to consider the various lines.

2.1. Although some British-type double-deckers ran on the early tramways in Paris, the majority of cars of the CGO were double-deck, single-ended vehicles of a totally different design. There was a commodious platform, with space for four standing passengers, a fairly easy stair and a knifeboard seat on the upper deck. The driver sat at the front of that deck and there was no front platform. This view is of an eight-window car, of the type first introduced in 1874, passing the Louvre, the upper deck apparently then the preserve of top-hatted gentlemen.

PARIS. — Colonnade du Louvre.

2.2. On a fine summer day there are parasols on the upper decks of these two horse cars passing in the boulevard du Temple.

1246. PARIS — Boulevard du Temple

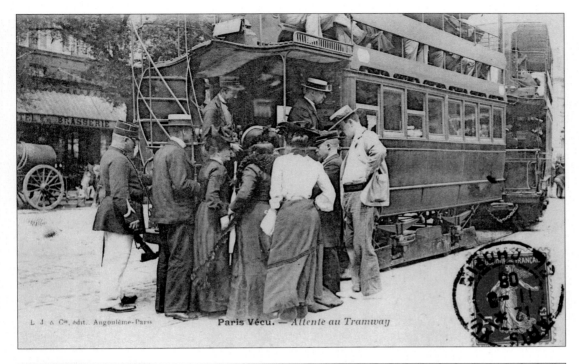

Paris Vécu. — Attente au Tramway

2.3. Fixed stopping places were introduced when mechanically-powered trams came into service and the CGO operated a system of queue tickets at busier stops, these being checked by an inspector before passengers were allowed to board. In this case, on a card posted in 1908, it would seem that there was a problem and the conductor looks on apprehensively. The tram is a former horse car in use as a trailer behind a double-deck motor car, the type of which cannot be ascertained.

6. BILLANCOURT — Route de Versailles

2.4. Prior to 1910, the only conventional electric trams operated by the CGO were those used on the long line TAB from Louvre to Versailles, electrified in 1906. Two are seen here with trailers on reserved track in Billancourt. At this point current collection was by overhead wire and trolley pole but when the trams reached Porte de Saint-Cloud, the trolley had to be hauled down and they were then ignominiously towed to their destination by (at first) compressed air locomotives and, when the task proved to be too much for these, by steam tram engines.

2.5. A view of the terminus outside the Gare de l'Est, between 1900 and 1910. Two double-deck compressed-air cars of the CGO negotiate the terminal loop before returning to Montrouge on line TG, one of the busiest on the system. They have the standard body fitted to all the mechanical trams of the CGO. The horse car on the left is bound for Gare du Nord on line TAH and behind it is the building housing the ticket office and commodious waiting room.

227 PARIS. — La Gare de l'Est. — LL.

2.6. The second view would have been taken c1914, just before the station would see crowds of young men setting off for the front and crowds of tearful relatives saying good-bye, an event now beautifully commemorated by a mural in the station. Trams now run across the front of the station and a G class motor car and A class trailer pause to pick up passengers. The Métro has reached this point and the classical entrance by M Cassien Benard can be seen on the right. The waiting room has gone. A taxi approaches the camera and behind it is a horse-drawn railway van. Behind that is a horse-drawn bus with much luggage on its roof, possibly run by the Chemin de fer de l'Est whose terminus this was.

66   East Station
         PARIS.— La Gare de l'Est   F. F.
                                             PARIS

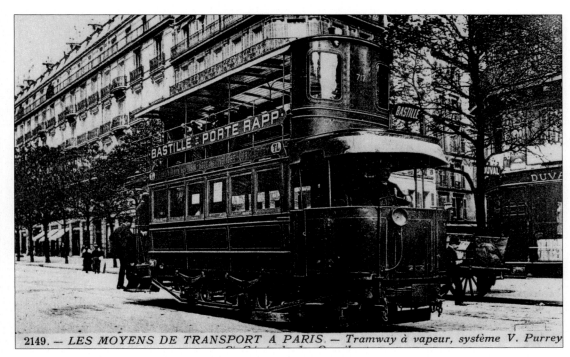

2149. — *LES MOYENS DE TRANSPORT A PARIS.* — *Tramway à vapeur, système V. Purrey*

2.7. The Bordeaux engineer Valentin Purrey devised a steam engine which was much lighter than those of the Serpollet design and enabled the weight of a double-deck tram to be kept down to 9.7 tonnes. The CGO acquired at least 50 double- and 36 single-deck Purrey cars, though the manufacturer's records give the total as 98. These trams were probably the most successful of all the mechanically-powered cars used in Paris and lasted until 13 June 1914. No.717 is in the boulevard de Saint-Germain.

3083 *PARIS — Le Théâtre Sarah-Bernhardt.* — *ND Phot.*

2.8. An accumulator car of line TF, inbound from Vincennes to Louvre via the quays, pauses at place du Châtelet. These 85 cars were built in 1900. Forty-five, which worked fairly well and sometimes pulled a trailer, were built by the Société Alsacienne in Belfort. The balance came from the firm of Fives-Lille and as these had difficulty pulling themselves up even the modest gradient in the rue du Faubourg Saint-Antoine, trailers were out of the question. Behind, a horse car makes for the Pont au Change and a double-deck trailer can also be detected. Built in 1874, the theatre was acquired by the actress Sarah Bernhardt in 1899 and duly renamed. It became the Théatre de la Cité under the Vichy régime, as she was thought to have had Jewish ancestry, and is now the Théatre de la Ville.

2.9. A rear view of a Purrey steam car working on line TD at place des Ternes. The inspector checks queue tickets. Behind is the Guimard entrance to the Métro station of line 2.

PARIS. — La Place des Ternes, l'Entrée du Métropolitain. — ND Phot.

2.10. Tram no.504 of the CGPT comes out of Ivry depot prior to taking up service on line 42 from Ivry to Châtelet. In every respect this tram is identical to preserved no.505 and would probably often have sat beside that car in the depot. The first depot at Ivry was one of four opened in 1877, three of which were replaced in 1907 by a large new complex on this site, with a capacity for 140 trams. On 6 November 1933 it was closed to trams and reopened as a bus depot on 14 April 1934. From 1950 to 1966 it also housed trolleybuses and it is still in use for buses, now known as Quai-de-Seine Ivry.

69. LE PETIT IVRY
Le Dépôt des Tramways   C. M.

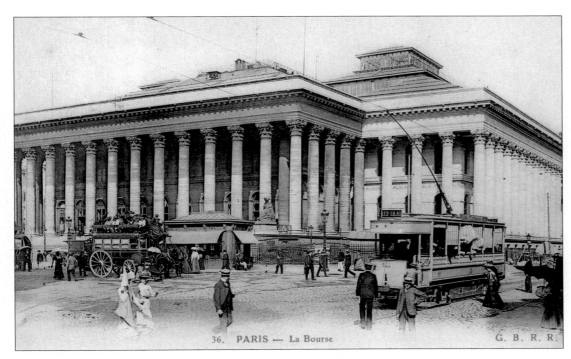

36. PARIS — La Bourse   G. B. R. R.

2.11. Semi-open tram no.511 of the Est Parisien passing the Bourse, en route from Opéra to les Lilas in the north-eastern suburbs. This line, 5, was electrified in 1905 and subsumed into other lines in 1909. There were twelve trams of this class, built in 1904 and laid out for second class only, perhaps more suited to a seaside resort than suburban Paris. They ran on maximum traction bogies.

30. - PARIS. - Théâtre du Châtelet et Colonne de la Victoire

et Cie, 61, rue de Rivoli, Paris

2.12. Double-deck bogie car no.204 of the CGPT at Châtelet, working to Malakoff on line 13 from les Halles (someone has forgotten to change the destination board). Sixty trams of this design were built in 1901 and most lasted into STCRP days. They were mounted on maximum traction bogies and had a capacity of 60 passengers. In 1921 or 1922 one disgraced itself by running away and overturning at Issy-les-Moulineaux; fortunately there was no one on board at the time.

2.13. Apart from no.398 of the CGPT, there is only horse-drawn traffic on the boulevard du Montparnasse in this view, taken early in the 1900s. It is all very leisurely and the conductor has time to view the scene from the end platform. These small cars were not at that time fitted with trolley poles and could run only on lines with side conduit; this one is working on that from Bastille to Gare du Montparnasse.

2.14. No.508, a 500 class tram of the Est Parisien, also working to les Lilas, negotiates the octroi gates at the Porte de Romainville.

4214. AUBERVILLIERS — La Place, La Mairie, l'Eglise et le Terminus des Tramways
E. M.

2.15. Two double-deck trams of the TPDS at the terminus of Mairie d'Aubervilliers, on a card posted there in 1919. These double-ended bogie cars were specific to this service and that to Pantin. The inner terminus was at place de la République and from electrification in 1898 the trams used trolley pole collection outwith Paris and accumulators from the city boundary to that terminus.

TOUT PARIS

798 — Rue de Belleville
(XIXe arr^t)
COLLECTION L. FLEURY.

2.16. A cyclist hitches a ride up the rue de Belleville from a cable car set. Given that the gradient was in places 70mm/m, any assistance was no doubt gratefully received. On the right there is a large photographic emporium and an equally large hat shop on the other side of the street. Next to the latter is what seems to be a public wash- and bath-house, probably much appreciated by the locals, few of whom would have had a bathroom at home.

2.17. A view of the cour du Havre of the Gare Saint-Lazare, looking up the rue d'Amsterdam. Two compressed-air trams of the CGO are working on line TAD from cour de Vincennes to Saint-Augustin while two of the then-new double-deck buses of type P2 are in the rue d'Amsterdam, on the line between Montmartre and Saint-Germain-des-Prés. As the bus on the left does not have a wind-screen on the upper deck, the view must have been taken between June 1906 and June 1907, when these were fitted to the fleet. Upper-deck passengers would no doubt have felt the full wind-tunnel effect as the vehicle dashed down from place Clichy. The artist has reproduced the livery of the buses fairly accurately but has gone badly wrong with the trams, which appear to be chocolate-brown instead of dark green.

2.18. A second view showing the same place between 1919 and 1921, with a G class motor car and an A class trailer on the same line, now numbered 26. There are a few motor vehicles around, although an elegant open carriage is about to cut across in front of the tram. The bus in the courtyard is a member of the Schneider H class, first built in 1916.

188. PARIS — Place de l'Ecole Militaire   G. B. R. R.

2.19. Co-existence at the junction at École Militaire, pre-1914. The double-decker is a compressed-air car of the CGO working on line TAF from Saint-Augustin to Montrouge, while single-decker no.585 of the CGPT is using electric power, on the side conduit system, on line 2 from Montparnasse to Étoile. A CGO horse bus completes the picture. On the left are two waiting rooms, presumably one for the passengers of each company.

504 PARIS. — Le Ministère des Colonies — LL

2.20. Compressed air car no.54 passes the Colonial Ministry en route from Hôtel de Ville to Passy on line TJ.

2.21. Another terminal station was the Gare Montparnasse of what was then the Chemins de fer de l'Ouest, familiar to thousands who came from Brittany and Normandy to seek their fortune in the capital, perhaps by working on the building of tunnels for the new Métro. The two single-deck trams are 300 class cars of the CGPT on the line from Bastille. A horse bus is dealing with passengers in front of the station and an elegant open carriage, with a smart horse, awaits its owner – but what is the curious four-wheel object just in front of it. Can it be one of these new motor cars? The handsome lines of the old station are in stark contrast to to-day's concrete monstrosity.

366 PARIS (XVᵉ). — La Gare Montparnasse. — LL.

2.22. Two classes of tram at the terminus of Courbevoie, on a card posted in 1908. The double-decker on the left, a Heilmann car of 1897, belongs to the TPDS and has come from Étoile. These trams were single-ended and ran on accumulator power only, each suburban terminus being provided with a power point from which the driver could top up the battery during layover. This operation required ten to fifteen minutes. The single-decker is on line 3 of the TMEP, which passed through Courbevoie en route from Pierrefitte and Saint-Denis to Saint-Cloud.

25 COURBEVOIE — Boulevard Bineau

H. S. A.

316. ~ PARIS. ~ Avenue de la Grande-Armée

2.23. It is hard to connect the elegant surroundings of the Arc de Triomphe with steam trams, but these did run beside it, using the tracks of the Nord company, later the TPDS. The trams were those of the Compagnie des Tramways à vapeur de Paris à Saint-Germain, on which service began in 1890. However, from Courbevoie inwards to the terminus at Étoile fireless locomotives were used and from 1902 this section was worked by the TPDS. Bound for Courbevoie, No.5 pulls two trailers along the avenue de la Grande Armée between 1902 and the electrification of the line in 1911. On the left is one of the pavilions designed by Hector Guimard for the entrances to line 1 of the Métro at Étoile.

11926 — NOISY-le-GRAND — Station terminus du Tramway   ES.

2.24. The terminus of the Nogentais line at Noisy-le-Grand before 1914, when that area was then still semi-rural. One of the 54-seat double-deckers, no.9, in original condition, waits to return to Porte de Vincennes, the destination being given simply as "Métropolitan". Trams of this class were later modernised with enclosed upper decks and were the last double-deckers to run in Paris, being withdrawn in 1929. A handsome gas lamp lit up the station after dark and to its right is an attractive brick waiting room. If a little refreshment was needed after a long tram ride, the Bar Terminus could provide just what was wanted.

2.25. Traffic conditions in the mid-1920s. This view was taken at Saint-Lazare, looking up the rue de Rome. Congestion is not too severe and the G class motor tram and A trailer on line 42, Saint-Denis – Madeleine, are having a fairly clear run on the last part of the journey. However, an ominously large number of buses, all Schneider H class, are lurking around.

2.26. This second view was taken rather later, probably c1930, and looks up the boulevard de Denain to Gare du Nord, whose stonework has not as yet been cleaned. A plethora of motor cars and a van seem to be milling around the intersection and the driver of the tram on line 21B, having fought his way through from Opéra, is no doubt glad to have disentangled his car and make off for the quieter environment of Pavillons-sous-Bois. The tram is a modernised car of class E' of the Est Parisien.

Chapter 3
Line T1 « Le retour du Tramway »

Although the revival of the tram in France dates back to 1975, it was some time before serious consideration was given to introducing it in the capital. It was first suggested for what is now line T1 in a report by Sofretu, a filial of the RATP, in 1975, but this did not lead to any action at the time, as the RATP saw articulated vehicles and bus corridors as the answer to the heavier flows of traffic on surface lines. Unfortunately for the bus, the proposals for a wide network of such corridors were met with a good deal of opposition, partly because roads were the responsibility of the Directions Départementales de l'Équipment (DDE). It seemed to many that the corridors would take up too much space and do little for the environment, while not providing a service of sufficient quality to attract passengers. Although bus lanes were ultimately established at a number of sites, such as those in Gennevilliers, these were fairly short and disjointed and to-day only the Trans Val-de-Marne busway in the south-eastern suburbs shows what the RATP intended to create in the 1970s. In 1976 the revised Schéma directeur proposed a network of 200km of reserved track lines at a distance of 5km from the boundary of Paris, including one along the road RD186, as and when that was relieved of some of its traffic by the opening of the parallel A86 motorway. It did not specify the type of vehicle to be used but the idea of a tramway between la Défense, Saint-Denis and Bobigny (capital of Seine – Saint-Denis) was proposed in 1977 by the Institut d'Aménagement et d'Urbanisme de la Région Parisienne (Institute for Urban Improvement in the Paris Region), along with a similar line in the south. The Institut quite deliberately used the word "tramway", although it was still considered old-fashioned by some, because the-then popular "métro léger" (light métro) meant little to most people. The RATP, however, was still not in favour of the idea. The plan for the former line was taken up with enthusiasm by the Council of Saint-Denis after the local elections of 1981, with the support of the Secretary for Transport (1981-1984), Charles Fiterman (Communist). In due course the Council managed to convince the RATP that a tram line along the RD186 between Saint-Denis and Bobigny would be a viable proposition and that it

would attract more traffic than would other modes of transport. It would also connect the termini of three recent extensions of the Métro, line 5 at Bobigny, line 7 at la Courneuve and line 13 at Saint-Denis. The area to be traversed appeared somewhat run-down and was losing population as industries closed and the proposed line therefore acquired something of a social character. The other local authorities were cautious, but it has to be remembered that, at this time, no modern street tramway had opened as new anywhere in Europe and planners could work only from models. In 1982 the RATP and the DDE launched a joint feasibility study on the project, looking at both estimates of the comparative costs of tram, articulated bus and articulated trolleybus and also the ability of each of these to attract traffic and the verdict of this study was on all counts in favour of the tramway. Finally on 28 October 1983 the proposal was adopted by the RATP board, this being followed in April 1984 by agreement of the STP.

A public enquiry was then held and a Déclaration d'utilité Publique (DUP) was issued on 19 December 1984, followed by formal adoption of the plan by central government in 1985. Finance was now secured, with 50% coming from government, 42% from the Région and the balance from the Département. The total cost (at 1984 figures) was to be FF520m (€79.3 million) and a date of 1988 was forecast for the opening. The rolling stock would be financed by RATP. As originally conceived the line was 9.1km long and served 22 stations, running from Saint-Denis (Gare SNCF) to Bobigny, Pablo Picasso. It was expected that trams similar to those being built for Nantes would operate it. Frequency in the peak periods would be a tram every four minutes and a passenger total of 55,000 per day was calculated. In committing itself to this level of support, the government was clearly nailing its colours firmly to the mast. Many experts in the field of urban transport predicted that the line would not attract the estimated number of passengers and that it would not fit in to the locality.

However, other administrative problems then arose. Inflation had pushed up the estimated cost to FF535 million (€82.30 million) plus about FF140 million (€21.53 million) for the trams and economies

had to be made. The Région was now lukewarm and managed to convince central government that it would be sensible to reconsider using buses. The RATP had to refine its calculations and in June 1987 presented a further report to the Secretary for Transport, now Jacques Douffiagues, stating that it would still prefer a tramway, this being supported with new figures. By that time, the tramway in Nantes had been successfully running for 18 months and that in Grenoble was on the point of opening. This report seems to have convinced the national politicians, in particular M Jean-Claude Gayssot (Communist), a deputy from Saint-Denis and later to be Minister for Equipment and Transport in the government of M Lionel Jospin, 1997-2002. On 21 July 1988 the first tranche of finance, FF110 million (€16.92million) for the construction of the line was unblocked by the Fonds de Développement Économique et Sociale. Relocation of public utilities began in April 1989 and in May of the following year, work started on the line itself.

Those involved in its construction were clearly under great pressure to make it a success. The major projects were the construction of two bridges, the first to take trams over the A1 motorway to the west of la Courneuve and the second to allow them to cross the tracks of the Grande Ceinture railway line between Hôpital Avicenne and Gaston-Roulaud. Two major hospitals were to be served, that just mentioned and the Hôpital Delafontaine, on the eastern edge of Saint-Denis. There were few problems associated with construction of the tramway and the RATP was careful to keep the public fully informed about what was happening. The line was finally opened from Bobigny to la Courneuve on 6 July 1992 and on to Saint-Denis on 21 December of the same year. In the event, it was somewhat over budget, by FF94 million (€16.46 million), and supplementary finance had to be obtained. A large programme of urban improvement was carried out by the Département of Seine-Saint-Denis. Under the direction of architect Paul Chemetov, façades along the route were improved, many trees were planted and street furniture specially designed for the project installed. The use of high quality "noble" materials, granite and cast iron, all indicated a project of a high

21

3.1. Publicity for the new tram line mentioned its advantages of silence, comfort and accessibility

standard and were used to back up the image which, it was hoped, the new tramway would convey. As first placed in service, line T1 had no common sector with the former tramways, save for a short section in Saint-Denis.

The success of the line surprised all those who had been involved with its construction, whether as supporters or critics, and delighted the former. The estimated number of passengers for the first year was attained after only a few months of service and the total continued to grow. Naturally, having spent so much on the new line, the authorities wanted to know what its users thought of it and enquiries into its use were therefore held in 1993 and 2000. Four counts of daily passenger numbers were taken between these years and the figures returned were of 60,000 in 1993 and 80,000 in 2000, an increase of 33%, with the greatest increase (65%) being in travel in off-peak hours, among those travelling to school and for leisure or shopping. In the peak periods, the increase was 36% in the morning and 42% in the evening peak and, given the urban geography of the areas served by the line, there was a fairly even spread in each direction at these times. Passengers who had previously used the bus for the same journey reported a gain of 9.3 minutes on average. To put these figures in context, it should be mentioned that over the same period, bus use had increased by 10% in Paris and 17% in the suburbs. A poll held among passengers in February 1993 revealed that users were very satisfied with the new form of transport, with comments such as "Le mode de transport idéal" and "Agréable comme le bus, efficace comme le Métro" (As pleasant as the bus, as efficient as the Métro). A similar exercise in 1995 showed that passenger satisfaction for the tram was 74% , while for the suburban bus it was 57%. The main advantages given for it were security, cleanliness, ease of use and information. There could be no doubt of the all-round success of the new tramway and, for those who had fought hard for it and in some cases staked their professional reputation on it, this must have come as a considerable relief and also brought a good deal of pleasure.

There was a penalty to be paid for this success, as the track paving began to break up under the stress of the frequency of service and it had to be replaced on the busiest stretches in the years 2006 to 2010. The new paving incorporates prefabricated panels designed to lessen vibration.

As a result of this success, plans were developed in 1998 for an extension of 2.9km with five stations, running east then south from Bobigny to Noisy-le-Sec, serving numerous educational and sporting establishments in the area and improving links from the east to the administrative capital of the Département. Trams would also connect at Noisy with the future line E of the RER (opened in 2000). The DUP was issued in April 1999 and work went ahead but there were problems in Noisy itself, where the avenue de Galliéni had to be widened in an operation which took some time, local businesses suffering in consequence. Finally the new section opened for service on 15 December 2003. Again the major work was a bridge, this one over the Canal de l'Ourcq. The cost of this extension was €80.95 million. With its opening, passenger numbers rose to 100,000 per day. In le Petit-Noisy, this extension revived a short section of former line 95 of the TPDS.

As first opened, line T1 ran in an almost-straight line on a north-west to south-east alignment across the north-eastern suburbs. The extension to Noisy brought a curve to the south. Its length was now 12km and there were 27 stations, of which five provided interchange with either the Métro or the RER and the suburban railways. With the first of these there are interchange points at Bobigny (line 5), la Courneuve (line 7) and Saint-Denis (line 13, with a walk of 250m), while with the RER and the Transilien suburban lines there is easy interchange at Noisy (line E) and at Saint-Denis (line D). At Bobigny there is a large suburban bus station. Apart from a short section in Saint-Denis, the entire line is on-street reservation and headways are five minutes off-peak and four minutes in the peak periods, with an average speed of 16km/hr, a figure that compares very favourably with the average speed of the buses which formerly ran on this route and managed only 13.5km/hr.

No depot was required for the line at that time, as the trams were shedded at the Bobigny depot of Métro line 5, whose workshop facilities they share, these having been extended to deal with the trams.

In 2000 proposals were first examined for a 4.9km extension of line T1, with ten additional stations, from Saint-Denis westwards to Asnières-Gennevilliers-les-Courtilles. The rather awkward terminus on the canal bridge at Saint-Denis had been laid out to allow for this without the need for rebuilding. The DUP was issued in 2006, after a favourable verdict from a public enquiry held between 12 December 2005 and 27 January 2006. The scheme was approved by STIF on 13 December of the latter year. Work began in 2008, the main project being the renovation of the two bridges at Saint-Denis. On the Île-Saint-Denis, there is some mixed running with general traffic, with priority measures for the trams, while at Gennevilliers and la Garenne-Colombes, the line uses pre-existing busways. It serves a densely-populated area, with a total of 157,000 residents in the communes concerned. There is interchange with RER line C at Gennevilliers and with line 13 of the Métro at le Luth. Construction went ahead steadily, to allow the extension to be opened on 15 November 2012 by M J-P Huchon. As the extension brought the trams beyond the boundary of Seine-Saint-Denis, he was able to praise it as "Un trait d'union" (a treaty of union) between the Départements 92 (Hauts-de-Seine) and 93 (Seine-Saint-Denis). A daily passenger total of 43,000 passengers is expected. The cost of the new section was €150.3 million (at 2008 prices), shared between the Région (53%), the Département of Hauts-de-Seine (27%) and central government (20%).

At its meeting on 6 July 2011, the council of STIF approved a further extension of 6.4km westwards from les Courtilles to Petit-Colombes, crossing the Commune of Colombes from east to west and originally intended to provide interchange with SNCF suburban trains and line T2 at la Garenne-Colombes before terminating at place Louis-Aragon. There was considerable debate about the exact course of this line in the centre of Colombes where, to serve the railway station, it would have had to use the rather narrow and very busy rue de l'Agent-Sarre. However, the plans for the future métro Grand Paris Express, as released in mid-2011, removed the need for line T1 to reach Colombes station and instead its course will lie to the north of the centre of that commune, joining line T2 at Parc Pierre Lagravère and terminating at the intersection of les Quatre Chemins. There will be seven or eight stations on the new portion and its cost is forecast at €125-135 million, this figure not including the purchase of some property which may be necessary. The additional trams required will cost €37.5 million. Construction began in 2014, with opening planned for 2017 or 2018. Here also line T1 will follow the general course of the former line 66. At a future date there could be an extension to Nanterre and Rueil-Malmaison, although this section may at first be served by a busway.

From Noisy an extension of 7.7km southwards to Val-de-Fontenay was originally planned in 2000, to open in 2006. At the local elections of 2001, the Left retained its position, but the result was then annulled and in 2003, at a new election, parties of the Right formed a majority in Noisy, with Nicole Rivoire (then UDF) as Mayor and leader of the opposition to the trams. Noisy then completely blocked the project, thus annoying the councils of Romainville and Montreuil and allowing the finance to be used elsewhere. Opposition centred on the narrow rue Jean Jaurès in Noisy, a vibrant street of local shops, and three possible options to solve this problem were put to the citizens in the summer of 2009. The favoured option was two-way running in that street and, with this point resolved, the extension was approved in principle by STIF on 8 July 2009. There was then another delay until a public enquiry was held between 17 June and 31 July 2013 and following this hearing, the project was recommended "Sans réserve" (without reservation). The DUP was issued on 17 February 2014. Work began in July 2015 and the opening of the line is planned for 2019. A passenger count of 50,300 passengers per day is expected.

Line T1 will in future be worked as two services, with a common terminus at Bobigny, where a four track station will be constructed, with cross-platform interchange between trams arriving from Saint-Denis and leaving for Val-de-Fontenay and vice-versa. There will also from 2022 be interchange with Métro line 15 at this point and at Pont de Bondy. Trams of line T1 will use the existing line to Noisy, from where there will be double-track in the pedestrianised rue Jean Jaurès. The first new station, Saint-Jean, will have a central island platform in the middle of the street and vehicle access will be restricted. The line will have 21 stations in all, of which 15 will be new, with interchange with RER line E and suburban rail services at Noisy, to which will be added the Tram Express Nord in 2017. At a later date, the line will connect with an extension of Métro line 11 at place Carnot. At its southern terminus, there will be interchange with RER line A and along the entire route there will be connexions with 18 bus lines. When Métro line 15 is opened, it will provide interchange at Rosny-Bois-Perrier and Val-de-Fontenay. A new depot and maintenance centre will be constructed at Murs-à-Pêches. The cost is expected to be €458.4 million, plus €45 million for the additional trams required and this will be funded by central government and the Région.

Rolling stock

In one sense, the administrative delays in approving the original line were fortunate, since, while the debate raged, the low floor tram of the type used in Grenoble (TSF2) had been developed by what was then GEC-Alsthom and it was clear that this design would offer a better choice for the new line than the Nantes design. A fleet of 17 cars (101-117) was therefore ordered and arrived in time for the opening of the first section. Unfortunately the growth in passenger numbers soon made this small fleet inadequate and a further two identical trams (118/9) were bought in 1995. As passenger numbers continued to climb, the enlarged fleet was no longer sufficient and in 2002/3, the 16 similar trams (201-216) used on line T2 were transferred to line T1, when the former line was re-equipped with Citadis vehicles. These trams have given excellent service and their modern design no doubt helped the Paris tram to get off to a good start. Originally they were painted in a livery of silver-grey with bands of white, blue and green running along the lower sides of the body, but they later adopted the RATP colours and became white with jade green window surrounds. By 2008 this rolling stock, although still running smoothly and quietly, was having some difficulty coping with peak-hour crowds and was considered to lack power to climb the gradients near place Carnot on the extension to Fontenay. It was also said by the opponents of that extension to be out-of-date. New trams will therefore be ordered for that section and the existing fleet will be confined to the more level western line. The success of line T1 has fully justified the faith of the planners, transport managers and politicians of twenty-five years ago.

Technical details TSF2 trams for lines T1 and T2

Length 29.40m, width 2.30m, 2 x 138kW motors, 174 passengers, 52 seated

References

Ville rail & Transports 28 January 2009 (extension to Val-de-Fontenay)

Publicity material issued by RATP.

3.2. Noisy-le-Sec looked very rural 110 years ago, when Est Parisien no.115 was inbound from Pavillons-sous-Bois to Opéra on line 3, a line opened in 1913. It was one of a class of trams brought into service in 1900, mounted on maximum-traction bogies. The body was divided into two compartments, first and second class, by an off-centre entrance and current collection was either, as here, by trolley pole or, in the inner sections of the line, by conduit. The road now forms part of dual-carriageway A3, no doubt using some of what was once the tramway reservation.

3.3. Nos 209 and 211 at Noisy terminus on 4 June 2005. The narrow rue Jean Jaurès, which has caused problems in the planning of the extension to Fontenay, can be seen behind the latter car.

3.4. No.109 crosses the Pont de Bondy on 3 May 2009.

3.5. When Bobigny was a terminus. No.107, in original livery, has just reversed on 5 March 1995.

3.6. No.108 nears Danton station in March 1997. New trees bring a touch of green to the neighbourhood.

3.7. The station of Basilique de Saint-Denis is somewhat cramped, due to its location between several tall, modern buildings. A crowd awaits No.116 in March 1997.

3.8. On the approach to the former terminus at Gare de Saint-Denis, trams run through the town centre on street track in the rue Delaune, from which other traffic is excluded. No.206 passes on 21 March 2015.

3.9. The terminus, on the bridge over the Canal de Saint-Denis, was awkward from the beginning and grew more and more unsatisfactory as traffic developed. However, on the damp Sunday morning of 5 March 1995, there were not many passengers awaiting the departure of no.117 for Bobigny.

3.10. It was a different matter twenty years later, on the afternoon of Saturday 21 March 2015. No.117 now carries the jade green and white corporate livery of the RATP.

3.11. A view of the square in front of Saint-Denis mainline station about 1905, with a single-deck tram awaiting departure for Pierrefitte. The line was opened in 1901 by the Compagnie des Tramways Mécaniques des Environs de Paris, trams running through from Saint-Cloud. The tram in this view is one of a batch of 30 central-entrance four–motor cars bought in 1901; these were the only four-motor cars to work in Paris. The line was ultimately numbered 65 and its inner terminus was moved to Porte de Clignancourt. It was replaced by buses in 1936. En route, this tram will follow much of the course of to-day's line T5.

71 SAINT-DENIS. — La Place de la Gare et la Rue du Port. — LL

3.12. No.205 emerges from the same (though rebuilt) bridge on 21 March 2015.

3.13. A view looking east from the Île-Saint-Denis on 29 June 2012. A tram at the former terminus can be seen through the bridge and publicity for the extension adorns the walls.

3.14. While the works for the extension were in progress at Mairie de Villeneuve-la-Garenne, buses serving the area were diverted quite some distance to the north of their usual route. However, a navette (shuttle service) was provided to cover the corridor to Saint-Denis. 3 May 2012.

3.15. At this point, the existence of a bus lane made conversion fairly easy. On 3 May 2013 all is in order once again and tram no.209 shares the road with Citelis bus no.8599, working on line 137 and displaying the new livery of STIF.

3.16. Nos.206 and 210 at Gennevilliers station on 3 May 2013.

3.17. Westbound trams run on to single track at Timbaud and from it directly through the centre of the old village. No.104 calls on the same date. Eastbound cars come in on the right after following a diversion around the village centre.

3.18. At the other end of the village, the west-
and eastbound tracks come together again
at the church of Sainte-Marie-Madeleine.
No.212 passes on 25 September 2013.

3.19. Publicity for the extension outside the
Métro station at les Courtilles on 29 June
2012.

3.20. Under a steady drizzle, alighting
passengers from no.107 at les Courtilles reach
for their umbrellas on 1 May 2013.

3.21. Line T1 is an entirely new line, with very little in common with the old tramways. However, at Asnières, it comes close to the former line of the TPDS, one of whose double-deck cars is seen at the terminus of line 66 in the Grand' Rue. The new line also revived short sections of former line 66 in Gennevilliers. The TPDS used one class of car for each main line and the trams used on this line were double-ended, double-deck bogie cars, capable of running on accumulators within Paris and on conventional overhead in the suburbs, as seen here.

A. D. Paris. — 4. — ASNIERES. — La Grande Rue.

3.22. An interior view of one of the TSF1 trams used on line T1.

3.23. A platform view at Bobigny in March 1995. The convenience of level boarding can be appreciated.

3.24. For the citizens of Montreuil, the extensions of Métro line 11 and tram line T1 cannot come soon enough; for the former they have been waiting since 1934. A poster displayed on the Mairie in September 2014 suggests that the government is not keeping its promises.

Chapter 4
Line T2 « La Ligne verte du Val de Seine »

Line T2 differs from T1 in almost every respect. For much of its length it runs on the trackbed of a former suburban railway line. It was built, after a good deal of wrangling and inter-company rivalry, by the Chemins de fer de l'Ouest. The line started at Champ de Mars and the section concerned began at what was then Issy-Plaine and terminated at Puteaux, where there was a connexion with the line to Versailles RD. It was opened without ceremony on 1 May 1889, the year of another international exhibition, which it was designed to serve, trains running between Saint-Lazare and Champ de Mars. Inter-company politics also played a part in the choice of route. The line was known as "La ligne des coteaux" (the line of the hills), referring to the hills which rise from the right bank of the Seine. From Issy there were intermediate stations at Bas-Meudon, Pont de Sèvres and Pont de Saint-Cloud, as well as three goods stations. South of Pont de Sèvres a new station was built at Bellevue-Funiculaire in 1893 and another was added at les Coteaux in 1900, to serve a housing development. Until 1914 the line carried a large amount of pleasure traffic but, apart from Sundays and holidays, it was never very busy and from 1913 trains started from and terminated at Issy.

Electrification on the 600V DC third rail system was completed on 22 July 1928, but little was done to improve the infrastructure and in 1933 the service became a shuttle between Issy and Puteaux . Traffic declined gradually over the years until the service was carrying no more than 5,000 passengers per day in 1983. Freight traffic, which had at one time been heavy, had ceased. The line was not converted to AC overhead operation when other lines in the western suburbs were so treated in the 1980s. Some trains of class Z5100, dating from 1951 and built for operation at 1,500V DC, were reduced to two coaches and converted for third rail operation at 750V by isolating one of the two motors on each motor bogie. This halved their power and they noisily and rather erratically kept the service going while the authorities debated its future. Those in the areas served were determined to update what many saw as a museum piece and to integrate it with its surroundings and the council of the Commune of Issy-les-Moulineaux had ambitious plans for sustainable commercial development, with some striking new buildings, many on the sites of former industrial activities. Coca-Cola, Hewlett-Packard and Johnson and Johnson were among the companies that decided to move to the area and a student hall of residence was also proposed. These plans have now been largely realised. The population of the commune grew with the increase in employment opportunities to 70,000 jobs. At the other end of the initial line, la Défense had grown to be a centre offering three million m² of office space.

After a joint study was undertaken by RATP and SNCF in 1979 there was general agreement that a tramway, with an extension to la Défense, was likely to be the best method of modernising the line and improving its usefulness to local communities. The length would be 11.7km. Various other forms of operation, such as a VAL line or connexion with RER line C, were considered but rejected. However, nothing happened for quite some time until the project was examined and given a favourable report by the STP in 1991. The DUP was obtained on 18 March 1993, the last train ran on 21 May and work began on the conversion. The track was completely replaced by welded rail, still to railway profile but laid out for right-hand running, overhead line was erected, the line voltage increased to 750, station platforms were lowered and several level crossings were closed. At Issy, now Issy-les-Moulineaux, where the track layout had to be altered, a metal viaduct was replaced by one in reinforced concrete and at Puteaux two new bridges had to be constructed and the layout changed to allow the line to continue to la Défense. The tunnel at Suresnes was lined in concrete. Seven new substations were built to supply current at 750V DC. As the trams would be driven on line-of-sight, the railway signals were abolished but new signals were installed at road crossings and at the entrance to sidings. Four new stations were constructed; at la Défense, Suresnes Belvédère, les Milons and Jacques-Henri Lartigue. Other stations were renamed; Bellevue became Brimborion, Pont de Saint-Cloud became Parc de Saint-Cloud, Pont de Sèvres became Musée de Sèvres and Bas-Meudon became Meudon-sur-Seine. It was in all a complex undertaking, not simply a case of substituting tram tracks for railway tracks.

It was planned to open the new line in 1995 but construction of the extension from Puteaux to la Défense was delayed by an action brought by the Mayor of that Commune, who took the SNCF to court over the expense of the conversion at Puteaux. After a legal process lasting in all 18 months the case was finally dismissed and the tunnel section could then be completed. The new trams were by that date out of guarantee and had to be insured, an expense not originally expected. The line was formally opened on 1 July 1997, with service beginning on the next day. There is interchange with line C of the RER at Issy Val-de-Seine, with line A and, in the future, line E of the RER, and Métro line 1 at la Défense and with suburban trains both there and at Puteaux. A new depot and maintenance centre was built to the south of Issy Val-de-Seine station. The total cost of the conversion and the extension to la Défense was slightly over original estimates at FF522 million (€80.30 million) (€7.1 million/km). The rolling stock cost FF250 million (€38.46 million). The infrastructure costs were met by central government (12%), the Région (57%), the Département of Hauts-de-Seine (14%) and by RATP and SNCF jointly (17%). The trams were funded by RATP alone.

As opened, line T2 was 11.7km long, with 13 stations. The average inter-station distance is 950m, allowing an average speed of 30km/hr and in some respects this part of the line is more of a tram-train than an urban tramway, but that description has not been used. The headway is 4 minutes in peak periods and 7-8 minutes in off-peak periods. Public enthusiasm for the new line was such that the trams rapidly became overcrowded. The number of daily users had been forecast as 27,000, possibly rising later to 36,000, but the former figure was exceeded by a considerable margin right from the start and a traffic count in March 1998 showed that 34,800 passengers were using the line every day. Of all users, 81% transferred to or from some other transport mode. In March 1998, 71% of those surveyed were travelling between the same points as they had done before the tramway opened. Of these, 10.55% formerly used a car, 85.5% used other public transport (30% bus), 2.55% walked, and the remainder used other means of transport. Of the total, 17% would not have made the same journey if it had not been by tram. This showed that 14.5% of the passengers were new users of public transport. By December 2004 the total number of passengers had risen to 71,530 and by 2009 to 83,000. Unlike line T1, this is a commuter's line with 85% of all passengers using it to travel to and from work or school, while only 15% are making optional journeys. Along with the success of line T1, these figures ensured that new tram lines would figure largely in the contract for the years 2000-2006 between the French government, the Région and the Départements concerned and they thus brought about the building of lines T3 and T4.

In the Seine, to the north of the present Musée de Sèvres station, there was once a small island, l'Île Rochellet. In the 17th century this was given by Louis XIV to his brother, the Duc d'Orléans, known as Monsieur, and consequently the island was renamed l'Île Monsieur. It became a royal pleasure ground where water pageants and sumptuous banquets were held. All this ceased with the first Revolution and the island was not restored to the royal family after 1815. In due course one channel of the river was filled in and the area passed to the Chemins de fer de l'Ouest and was used for the goods station of Sèvres-Saint-Cloud. Goods traffic gradually declined and the station was demolished in 1993. As built, line T2 ran directly through the area but in 2005, as a new leisure centre was constructed on the former island, it was necessary to divert the tramway between Musée de Sèvres and Parc de Saint-Cloud. The new section came into operation in two stages, on 27 November and 11 December 2006.

From the start of service it had been intended that Issy should not be the permanent terminus of the line and that it should at some date be extended eastwards, as far as Tolbiac, possibly by use of the trackbed of the former Petite Ceinture line, and as such it was mentioned in the plans for Orbitale and shown on maps of 1996. The latter option was finally discarded and in December 2006 work began on an extension of 2.7km to Porte de Versailles, with two intermediate stations and some street running, on reservation, on the approach to the new terminus. In late 2008 it was decided to add a third station at the new commercial area of Issy, since the nearest station would otherwise have been about 700m distant from the office block known as the Tour Mozart. This station, Henri Farman, would be used by 750,000 people per annum. It also serves the Paris héliport.

At the terminus, there is passenger interchange with line T3 and with Métro line 12. The former involves crossing a fairly busy road and has not been laid out as conveniently as passengers could have wished. Nor are the tracks of T2 and T3 connected. The large exhibition centre at Porte de Versailles provides much additional traffic on occasions such as the "Foire du Livre" (book fair) or the Salon annuel de l'Agriculture, both very popular events.

The first rails of the extension were laid in June 2008, trial running followed in the autumn and subsequently "marche à blanc", this allowing local people "à vivre avec le tramway et les nouveaux aménagements urbains" (to live with the tramway and the new urban arrangements). The extension opened for traffic on 21 December 2009. Ten new trams were required to carry the additional traffic and, including these, the total cost of the extension was €110.59 million. Unfortunately 120 trees had to be cut down, but 200 new ones were planted and the RATP was thus able to maintain its green credentials. Cycle paths were improved all along the extension. The terminus at Porte de Versailles is located on the site of the former terminus of lines 23 and 32 and some of the rails of the old system were still in place when work started on the new line.

There was also a plan that, at its northern end, line T2 should be extended from la Défense to Pont de Bezons and possibly beyond to Sartrouville and Val d'Argenteuil. This line would run along the route of the RD992, a road with two carriageways of three traffic lanes each, and used by 70,000 vehicles per day. In the event, the extension was terminated at Pont de Bezons, a distance of 4.2km from la Défense, with seven stations. It was to serve an area with 32,000 inhabitants and 29,000 employment places. A public enquiry was held between 7 March and 8 April 2005, the DUP was issued later that year and the project was approved by STIF on 13 December 2006. A new depot has been built at Colombes, on a short branch off the main line to a site formerly owned by the French navy and, at one time, intended to be the new home of the AMTUIR transport museum. Total cost was expected to be €277 million, but the line came in slightly under budget at €223.5 million (€49.5m/km) with €53 million for rolling stock . The cost was shared between the Région (66%), central government (18%) and the two Départements of Hauts-de-Seine and Val- d'Oise (16%). The RATP met the bill for the 18 new trams.

This was an expensive tramway but the area served is densely populated and much new residential building was undertaken to coincide with the extension. Local bus services, especially line 272, were crowded at all times of the day and desperately needed some relief. It was expected that 58,000 additional passengers per day would be attracted to the new service, which would have a headway of four minutes in peak periods. The line from la Défense to Bezons was once served by tram lines 62 and 63.

Preliminary work began in January 2009 and the first rails were laid in Colombes in April of that year. A great deal of infrastructure work was necessary, particularly at la Défense, where the line had to cross under the tracks of the Transilien suburban rail services and this tunnel had to be extended to place de Belgique in la Garenne-Colombes, just before Faubourg de l'Arche. The Pont de Bezons (1955), which is a listed structure, had to be rebuilt to take the tracks while still offering its former road capacity. To allow this, new paths for pedestrians and cyclists were constructed on each side of the bridge and to support these, six new arches had to be created to reinforce the original three of the bridge, without detracting from its appearance. All this was done, amid a certain amount of congestion, while the bridge remained open for traffic. The alterations to the bridge cost €7 million. These two factors, tunnel and bridge, were the main reason for the high cost of this extension. Although the RD992 had still to be wide enough to cope with dense traffic, there are now only two carriageways on each side of the tramway and the wide green areas on each side of the tracks have vastly improved the amenity of the area. The depot was opened on 22 June 2012 while service on the extension began on 19 November. No other tram line in Paris has, in the time since it was opened, seen equivalent changes in housing and commerce along its route and by 2014 line T2 was carrying 130,000 passengers per day.

Unusual and very interesting features of the stations on line T2 are the coloured panels giving details of events and people connected with it. There are five themes in all – the history of the tram (violet), people connected with the line or the names of the stations (light blue), the culture of the area (green), the environment (orange) and events and personalities (sea blue). All are worth detailed study and a visitor should allow plenty of time to read the panels before boarding a tram.

Depots

The depot and workshops for the first section of the line were built at Issy-les-Moulineaux, on the site of the former goods station. It has the advantage of being accessible at either end from the running lines. The maintenance centre has four roads, of which three are electrified and two have both pits and overhead gantries to allow the staff to work on equipment mounted on the roofs of the trams. Next to the centre is a washing plant. There are five open-air roads for stabling the cars and, in all, these can accommodate 20 trams.

The depot for the extension to Bezons is at Colombes and has the same facilities.

The control centre is located beside the depot at Issy-les-Moulineaux.

Rolling stock

The line was initially worked by a fleet of 16 TFS2 trams similar to those of line T1 but with certain adaptations, particularly with regard to fire safety in tunnel operation. The phenomenal growth of passenger numbers meant that these very soon became inadequate and these were replaced in 2002/3 by 26 larger Citadis trams of type 302. These at first operated solo but it soon became necessary to run them in coupled sets and to allow this to be done, platforms had to be lengthened. The first set ran on 5 September 2005. Sixteen additional trams of this type were subsequently ordered to cope with the additional traffic on the extension to Porte de Versailles. As there are short lengths where the trams meet road traffic, it was necessary to shroud the couplings, giving these trams a quite different appearance from earlier ones. Eighteen more trams of the same design were acquired for the northern extension and six more were ordered in 2014 for delivery in 2016, at a cost of €17.5 million, to be financed by STIF. These are at present the only trams in France to operate in coupled sets.

Technical details Citadis 302

Length 32.2m, width 2.40m, 4 x 140kW motors, 213 passengers, 48 seated.

References

Connaissance du Rail April-May 2010 nos.348/349

Ville & Transports 3 October 2007 (development of Issy)

La Ligne des Moulineaux. Pierre Bouchez. La Vie du Rail, Paris, 2008.

T2 Line diagram

4.1. By 21 September 2008 the ground had been cleared for the new terminus at Porte de Versailles.

4.2. The notice giving details of the new terminus, 3 May 2009.

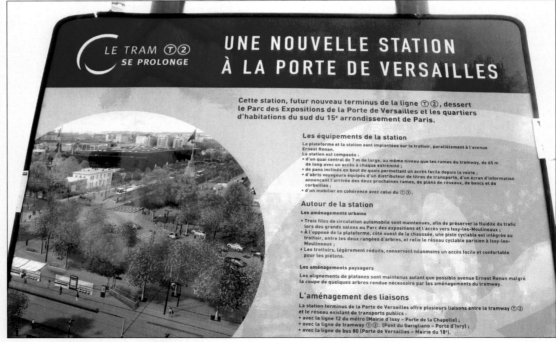

4.3. One year later, the frame of the station has been completed, but the finishing touches still remain to be added.

4.4. At 09.15, towards the end of the morning peak hour on 3 May 2013, the station is busy as no.440 prepares to leave, working as a short turn car to Issy.

4.5. The first works on the station then known as Porte de Sèvres, as looking east in May 2009.

4.6. The station was actually opened as Suzanne Lenglen. No.454 approaches on 22 March 2015.

4.7. Snow on the ground at Henri Farman as no.418 approaches on Monday 30 November 2010. The new office blocks, the raison d'être of this station, can be seen to the right.

4.8. On the afternoon of 13 October 1980, the surroundings of Issy-Plaine are gloomy and there is only one passenger for the rather sad little train of SNCF Standard stock about to leave for Puteaux.

4.9. A quarter of a century later, on 4 June 2005, the scene at what is now Issy-Val-de-Seine is more lively and the cranes behind no.411 testify to the upturn in the now-vibrant local economy.

4.10. The economy of the area around Meudon was originally based on the excavation of chalk for use in several industries, including the manufacture of cosmetics. However, in the late 19th century – and especially after the coming of the railway – it became an area that attracted many excursionists from the city and also some distinguished residents. Among these was the sculptor Auguste Rodin who arrived in 1893 and in 1908 moved into the villa which now houses the museum of his work. A panel at Meudon station gives details and also mentions that the poet Rainer Maria Rilke in 1903 came down to visit him by train from Montparnasse in just twenty minutes.

4.11. The area is still very pleasant and the old station building, at what is now Meudon-sur-Seine, has been preserved. No.416 calls on 22 March 2015.

4 — BELLEVUE. — Funiculaire

4.12. A view of the Meudon funicular from the appropriately-named station of Bellevue-Funiculaire (Brimborion). On the right is a train bound for Puteaux or Saint-Lazare and it includes both open-sided and enclosed doubled-deck coaches in its make-up. Accidents were common with the former and the last was replaced in 1931. The enclosed coaches, some of which ran until 1950, were nicknamed "Bidels" as it was thought that the passengers crowded behind the barred windows bore a passing resemblance to the monkeys in the cages of M Bidel's ménagerie. Such were the crowds of excursionists using the original station at holiday times that the station building soon proved inadequate and it was rebuilt and enlarged in 1900.

4.13. A view from almost the same spot to-day. In pouring rain on 18 September 2015 no.427 arrives, bound for Bezons. Trees now cover the course of the funicular,

4.14. Musée de Sèvres is one of the most attractive stations on the line. Here also the original station building has been carefully restored and now serves commercial purposes. The greenery is always meticulously tended. No.401 is northbound on 3 May 2013.

4.15. This panel gives full details of the history of l'Île Monsieur and also mentions that the very rare orchid *Centaura Leucophaea* has found a home in the new park.

4.16. The diversion of 2005 north of Musée de Sèvres involved some sharp reverse curves, one of which is being negotiated by no.449 on 18 September 2015.

4.17. Parc de Saint-Cloud gives access to the former royal/imperial park of that name and to a pleasant section of the right bank of the Seine. There is interchange with local bus lines at the bus station, on the right in this picture, and the station is usually busy, as when Nos.459 and 415 call on 3 May 2013.

4.18. Les Coteaux, shortly after electrification of the line in 1928. The train is being propelled headed by one of the "fourgon-moteurs" (motorised luggage vans) built for the Chemins de fer de l'Ouest in 1900 and consists of two-axle stock with end platforms. These ten Bo-Bo electric locomotives of 350kW were successful and, modernised, some lasted in service until 1951. The station has been completely altered, but the old building still straddles the tracks of line T2.

7. - LES COTEAUX (St-Cloud) — Intérieur de la Gare

4.19. Clear and distinctive signs direct passengers to the station from the surrounding streets.

4.20. On 3 May 2013 a southbound tram emerges from the short tunnel under Mont Valérie, on the approach to Sursenes station.

4.21. No.213 at la Défense, when this underground station was the northern terminus. (Jim D Schantz)

4.22. Beyond la Défense, the line becomes a street tramway and it emerges into an inner-suburban landscape, dominated by the towers of the business centre. However, as shown in this view at Faubourg de l'Arche, taken on 3 May 2013, it has brought a refreshing touch of green to the area.

4.23. The site of the future station, Jacqueline Auriol, looking towards la Défense, on 4 June 2011.

4.24. Just over a year later, on 29 June 2012, work on the station is well advanced and construction of other buildings in the vicinity is also progressing.

4.25. The station in service on 3 May 2013. Jacqueline Auriol (1917-2000) was famous not only as the daughter-in-law of President Vincent Auriol, but also as the first woman test pilot to fly a jet fighter in France. M Auriol was the first head of state of the Fourth Republic and Jacqueline married his son in 1938. It was largely thanks to his influence that she abandoned her intended career in design and took to the air instead.

4.26. Local authorities took advantage of the construction of the tramway to carry out other schemes of urban improvement, as seen on this poster at les Quatre Chemins in June 2012.

4.27. The buses of line 272, which the trams have replaced south of Bezons, were chronically overcrowded at all times, even, as here, on a Saturday afternoon. More passengers attempt to squeeze themselves on board Renault Agora no.2764 at les Quatre Chemins on 29 June 2012.

4.28. Boarding tram no.443 is easier. A scene at Victor Basch at mid-day on 3 May 2013. This station corresponds to the bus stop seen above, but is located on the other, south, side of the intersection. Victor Basch (1853-1944), was a professor at the Sorbonne who was also the chairman of the Ligue des Droits de l'Homme (League of the Rights of Man) from 1926 until he and his wife were murdered in Lyon in 1944 by thugs who supported the Vichy régime.

4.29. The depot under construction in June 2011.

4.30. Preliminary excavations to allow diversion of utilities and preparation of the track bed at Parc Pierre Lagravère on 18 September 2009. On the left, road traffic has been confined temporarily to a single lane for each direction.

4.31. By 4 June 2011 track and overhead are in position, and the foundations of the station have been laid. The emphasis on improving the environment by laying grass on the reservation and by the planting of many trees – a key aim of the architects Gautier and Conquet – is already evident. Both roads flanking the tramway are in service again but have been reduced from three to two lanes in each direction.

4.32. The station in service in May 2013. No.406 is bound for Bezons.

4.33. The density of motor traffic makes it difficult to photograph trams on the Pont de Bezons.

4.34. Nor was life easy for those keeping the bus services going and the traffic flowing while the line was being built over the bridge. On 4 June 2011, Renault Agora no.2770 approaches Bezons on line 272, while behind an older vehicle, an R312, follows on line 163.

4.35. To-day trams have priority on the approach from the bridge to the terminus. A coupled set leaves the terminus on a southbound trip.

4.36. The terminal station has been laid out to provide cross-platform interchange with buses and a short section of reservation allows these to work "wrong line" to allow this. A busy scene on 3 May 2013.

4.37. The construction of the line was in no small measure due to the enthusiasm and hard work of Jacques Leser (Communist), Mayor of Bezons from 1979 to 2001 and a councillor of Val d'Oise for 19 years. Sadly, he died on 15 February 2012 and so did not live to see the opening of the extension. In his eulogy, M Dominique Lesparre, his successor as Mayor, cited the tramway as one of the finest examples of his work for the Commune and this memorial at its terminus ensures that his efforts are not forgotten.

Jacques LESER
1936 – 2012
Maire de la
Mairie de Bezons
1979 – 2001

Initiateur de l'arrivée
du tramway sur la ville
et de la mobilisation
des Bezonnais pour l'obtenir.

Chapter 5
Line T3 « La Ligne pour tous »

The success of lines T1 and T2 greatly influenced the decision to include extensions of these lines and the construction of other new tram lines in the contract between central government and the Région for 2000-2006.

The ancestry of this line is again totally different from that of the two previous lines. From the mid-19th century Paris was served by the Petite Ceinture circular railway line, the first section of which was opened in 1852. It was run by a syndicate of the main-line railway companies. At first only freight trains used the line but from 1862 passengers were also carried and after the circle had been completed in 1867, this traffic became very important. The opening of the first stage of the Métro in 1900 and the later development of the motor bus and electric tram took away much of the line's traffic, which had declined to about 5 million passengers per year by 1930. There was no attempt at modernisation or co-ordination with these newer forms of transport and, post-1918, no one seemed to have any interest in its future. After some half-hearted attempts to persuade the CMP to take it over, which were met by equally weak excuses for not doing so, the passenger service was replaced in July 1934 by buses running on the boulevard des Maréchaux as line PC. The change was much welcomed by the public. The railway remained open for freight and transfer passenger traffic and the section between the Gare du Nord and Gare de Lyon became well known to tourists as the route taken by through coaches from Calais to southern destinations.

After 1920 the boulevard des Maréchaux gradually became a main motor road, the double row of trees was destroyed and underpasses were constructed at many of the former gates to speed the flow of traffic. Between 1958 and 1973 the boulevard périphérique was built on the suburban side of the former wall but, with the growth of motor traffic, the inner ring remained a main traffic artery. The PC bus service, greeted with so much enthusiasm in 1934, became less and less attractive, as it was subject to long delays due to increasing traffic congestion. At the various gates, it crossed the main flows of traffic entering or leaving the city and the problem was most acute at these points. The service was later split

into three separate lines, denoted PC1-PC3, but that could not by itself solve the problem.

In the 1950s, when the RATP had a brief flirtation with the trolleybus, there was consideration of converting the PC service to trolleybus operation and definite plans were made for the section between Porte d'Orléans and Porte de Vincennes. Some masts were even erected to support the overhead but official enthusiasm cooled rapidly and the motorbuses continued unchallenged.

By 1993 the three bus lines were transporting 130,000 passengers per day, using articulated buses, while the former railway now saw little traffic, the freight trains having been withdrawn in that year and transfer traffic having ceased. In that year also, when the extension of T2 to Porte de Versailles was first mooted, the RATP sought clarification on the proposal that this should be further extended to Porte d'Ivry, along the trackbed of the line, which still belonged to RFF, to replace part of the PC bus service. A depot would be built on the site of the former railway goods yard at Gobelins. The authorities generally supported the idea, and in 1995 the STP asked the RATP and the SNCF to study the building of a tramway through this area, either using the former railway formation or running on the boulevard des Maréchaux or on a combination of the two. This study showed that use of the railway formation would give a line 7.7km long , with 13 or 14 stations and would allow the fairly high average speed of 28km/hr but, as much of the southern section of the line is on embankments, interchange with the Métro would not be easy and a great deal of money would have to be spent to make the stations fully accessible. It was forecast that 1,700 passengers would use the line each hour. The cost, at 1996 prices, would be FF1.8 milliard (€27.69 million). Placing the line on the highway would cost slightly more (FF2.1 milliard, €32.1 million) and would result in the lower service speed of between 15 and 17km/hr, but there could be 17 stations and access and interchange would be much easier. It was calculated that many more passengers, probably between 1,900 and 2,000 per hour would be attracted to it. Objections were voiced (loudly) by many of those who lived along the line of the Ceinture and, had it

been used, it would probably have been necessary to place much of the line in a cutting or tunnel, greatly increasing the cost of construction as well as making the journey less attractive to passengers. Placing it on street would also allow the local authorities to carry out various schemes of urban improvement and introduce traffic management to reduce the volume of motor vehicles using these roads and thus improve the quality of life for residents of the area. The debate went on for several years and, as RFF was somewhat intransigent, it became fairly acrimonious. On 7 July 1998 a diesel railcar carried a group of politicians and officials on a study tour of the former rail line and plans were then published for two tram-train services, one to run from la Défense via T2 and then via the Ceinture to Porte de Charenton, with a branch from there to Bercy. The second would start at either Bibliothèque Francois-Mitterrand or possibly Gare d'Austerlitz and run to Porte de Clichy. The Mayor of Paris from 1995 to 2001, Jean Tiberi (RPR), who proposed to create a green corridor along the line of the Ceinture, favoured this version of the plan and ensured that the line was listed in the contract between the government and the Région for 2000-2006.

However in the local elections of 2001 M Bertrand Delanöe (Socialist) became Mayor and, with the support of the Greens, rejected that proposal in favour of the street running solution. He considered that the sharing of public space and an associated reduction in the use of the car to be "Un enjeu de civilisation" (a crucial aspect of civilisation). The line was now envisaged as a self-contained operation, rather than as part of T2, and would run from Pont de Garigliano in the west to Porte d'Ivry in the south-east, a distance of 7.9km. It would be entirely on its own right-of-way, meeting road traffic only at junctions. The cost was now given as €185.2 million, this being financed by the national government (16.3%), the Région (26.1%), the city of Paris (30.1%) and the RATP (27.5%), the last of these having also to finance the construction of the 21 trams necessary to work the line, at a cost of €51.2million. The many associated works on the road system and on urban improvement took the final cost to €311.3 million, making this one of the most expensive tramways in France, at almost €40 million/km. In the case of the rolling stock, the finance actually took the form of a loan from the Région, at a non-commercial rate. The RATP and the City's Direction de la Voirie (Roads Department) were themselves responsible for the management of the entire project and M Denis Baupin of the latter drove the project forward with unquenchable enthusiasm. It was no easy task, as it involved liaison with 300 contractors and the authorities of nine arrondissements within Paris and several suburban communities such as Ivry, Montrouge and Issy. Legally the powers to build the line were exercised under the Law Laure, (Law of Air Quality), December 1996.

A public enquiry was held between February and April 2003 and construction work began in the middle of that year. After two months of trials, the line was inaugurated on 16 December 2006, almost exactly five years from the date when the STIF agreed to the project. In his address, the Mayor[1] not only looked back with pride on what had been achieved but also looked forward to a time when the benefits of a modern tramway would be available to many more inhabitants of the suburbs, with an extension of T3 to Porte de la Chapelle. Some local politicians unfortunately chose to boycott the ceremony and there was a brief interruption of the proceedings by demonstrators. More peacefully, some other people used the occasion to make a statement against the new tramway in Jerusalem, saying "Merci" to T3 but "Non, merci" to a tramway for that city, as that line, now open, runs into illegally-occupied territories. The celebrations also included street theatre, by actors whose costumes of green and orange reflected two of the main colours used on the new line. These events brought the tram back in to the city area of Paris after an absence of over 68 years. Passenger service began the next day and over 100,000 people stormed, or in some cases attempted to storm, the trams to sample line T3.

The main bus termini, such as Porte d'Orléans, were upgraded with street furniture of the same quality as that of the tramway and rearranged to bring the buses nearer its stations. Five bus lines were altered to improve links between Paris and suburban communes. The various Métro stations at interchange points were upgraded to the same standard.

The line runs on its own right-of-way throughout

its length, flanked for most of its length by two lanes of traffic and cycle tracks on each side. The only exception to this layout is the section between Stade Charléty and Porte de Choisy, where the tracks are on the south side of the carriageway. On the original line T3, there are 17 stations, including the termini, of which six provide interchange with Métro lines 4, 7 (at two stations), 8, 12 and 13, and two with the RER, lines B and C. There is also interchange with the extension of line T2 at Porte de Versailles, as well as with 18 city and 19 suburban bus lines. Connexions with the truncated PC bus service are provided at each end of the line, although that at Pont de Garigliano is not well arranged, as passengers have to cross the carriageway of what is a fairly busy road. At the western end, the Hôpital Georges Pompidou provides a good deal of traffic, while Cité Universitaire is a particularly busy stop, serving a large student population. At certain times, sporting events at Stade Charléty and events in the exhibition grounds at Porte de Versailles lead to very high passenger numbers. Apart from some very short sections at termini, lines T3a and T3b have nothing in common with the former tramways.

Publicity for the new line and for the transformation of the boulevards was comprehensive and to a high standard. An information sheet, Le Journal du Tramway, was published every three months and this was backed up by a series of leaflets on particular aspects of the scheme, such as parking during the works.

The construction of the tram line was accompanied by a large-scale programme of urban improvement, the re-invention of the boulevard as envisaged by M A Alphand in the book Les Promenades de Paris of 1867. Under the direction of the architect M Antoine Grumbach, a team of landscape architects and planners, developed a "boulevard jardiné" (a garden boulevard). The central platform, on which the tramway runs, is grassed for its entire length to a width of 6 or 6.5m. Pavements are 8m wide and are planted with 3,500 trees. Along the length of the pavements are service roads, to allow deliveries and outside these are the cycle tracks. Entries to side roads have a raised surface to slow down traffic entering these areas. The stations, designed by Agence Wilmotte, were designed to reflect the beauty of the tree and each has five, interspersed between the passenger shelters. The result has been that the character of the Maréchaux

has been totally altered from that of a main urban highway, with little greenery but many car parks, to one of a quieter road serving the locality. It has been quite a change.

To date the traffic on line T3 has exceeded all expectations, to the extent that the millionth passenger arrived long before the RATP was ready to welcome him/her. In its first complete year of operation the line carried 25 million passengers, an increase of more than 50% over the total carried annually by the PC bus service over the same route. By the end of 2007, traffic had reached the level of 110,000 passengers per working day and 70,000 per day at week-ends and holidays. Of these users, 52% were making a journey between Paris and a suburb or vice-versa, 7.4% a purely suburban journey and the remainder a local journey. A new record was set on 7 May 2010, during the Foire de Paris held at the exhibition grounds at Porte de Versailles, when trams ran well into the night and 147,851 passengers were carried, without any problems arising. On each of the next two days 120,000 people used the line. However, delays leading to bunching of the trams, did subsequently occur when large numbers were travelling and off-peak frequencies were therefore increased on 2 March 2009. On 6 and 7 April 2009 an experiment in increasing peak-period frequency was conducted, with 17 trams in service as against the normal 15. The information gained on such matters as the effect on other road traffic at signals will be used in future planning for the line. By the end of 2010, road traffic along the boulevards had decreased by 50% since 2006, with a consequent reduction of 40% in accidents.

Despite the success of line T3, the Cour des Comptes, which is charged with overseeing public expenditure, issued a report in 2009 severely criticising the decision to locate the line on the public highway rather than on the trackbed of the former railway. It was suggested that the cost had been too high and that the benefits had been exaggerated. This report appeared to take no notice of the fact that many journeys made on the trams are very short - something which can easily be confirmed by personal observation - and that the passengers concerned would have been unlikely to use widely-spaced stations, even if these had, at considerable cost, been made fully accessible.

---

1 M Delanoë had meanwhile instituted the system of Vélib (bicycles for hire) in Paris and it had proved to be very popular.

Depot and Workshops

The depot is situated on a short spur from place Balard in the rue du Général Lucotte. The complex houses a maintenance centre, the control centre, the driving school and a washing machine, through which trams run as they come out of service. Open air parking is used to store the trams.

Rolling stock

Service was initially provided by a fleet of 21 double-ended trams of Alstom's Citadis 402 type, numbered 301-321. These are seven-section cars, with 100% low floor configuration. The expected level of traffic decided the dimensions and their width makes these trams incompatible with those of line T2. Both internal and external design was studied very carefully by a team of specialist designers led by Mme R Charvet Pello of the firm of RCP design global. The interior colour scheme was prepared by the designer M V Hertig and the exterior scheme was by members of the firm of bdc conseil. These schemes were evolved to give an ambience which would be warm and welcoming and would, externally, suggest the elegance and flexibility of the tram. Each tram has its own internal decorative scheme in a combination of yellow, orange, green and turquoise. The material of the seats emphasises the tree, the new symbol of the boulevards. Each tram has a personalised external feature in the form of a jade green band, running below the windows and featuring illustrations of aspects of Parisian life such as the pavements, the traffic lights and the always-welcome cup of coffee. As the vehicles had to blend in with a very considerable scheme of environmental improvement, the end sections therefore feature a gently-tapered and very elegant cab front, to avoid any suggestion of threatening. After eight years of intense service, all these features are still as fresh and attractive as they were when the line opened.

Technical details

Length 43.7m, width 2.65m, 6 x 120kW motors, 304 passengers, 78 seated.

On 3 July 2009 RATP and Alstom jointly presented car 301 as modified to run on system STEEM[2]. The manufacturer had been working on the project since 2007 and no.301 was tested on the track at Alstom's factory at la Rochelle in the summer of 2008. It returned to its home city in December of the same year. Test running on line T3 followed early in 2009 and authorisation to use the car in passenger service was given in June of that year. It had been rebuilt to carry 48 modules of supercondensators, each weighing 15kg and, to provide space for these, one braking resistance had to be removed from the roof and the pantograph placed on a raised platform. The second part of the scheme was to create a rapid recharging centre at Lucotte workshops. This equipment can function either during braking, when the motors feed current to the condensators, or by charging for a brief period when the car is stationary. It allows the tram to run 400m at 30km/hr without overhead. The cost of the experiment was €4 million. The capacity of the condensators was increased in 2010 from 1.6kW/hr to 2kW/hr. The very low internal resistance allows quick recharging (in 20 seconds) and the process has been nicknamed "Biberonnage" (like a baby drinking from a bottle). Due to this feature, the supercondensators are much more suitable for frequent recharging than is a conventional battery. Although the results of the trials were "remarquables", according to M J-L Cibot, Rolling Stock Engineer of the RATP, it is not intended to convert existing lines to this form of operation, but to use it on new lines only. The choice of line T3 for the trials was due to its having all the characteristics of a busy tramway. It is estimated that it could lead to a saving in current of at least 15% and possibly up to 30%. Given that the RATP in 2010 paid €210 million for current, such a saving would be significant.

From 14 November to 10 December 2011, line T3 was used to test an experimental service of cargo trams. No actual cargo was carried, but a tram which did not carry passengers was inserted into the service during off-peak hours to test the practicality of the idea. It was calculated that a cargo tram could carry 80 tonnes of freight and so replace three semi-trailers. It seemed to be successful and economic studies followed in 2012, with a view to beginning such a service in the years after 2015, either on line T3 or on one of the new lines. The main customers would be large supermarkets or the market at Rungis on line T7. It would be necessary for the RATP to seek powers to run freight trams, since at present its legal status is that of a passenger carrier only.

Extensions

Given the success outlined above and the re-election of M Delanoë in 2008, it is not surprising that ambitious plans to extend the line were soon formulated and that these were enthusiastically received by local people. A consultation exercise had already been held between 30 January and 15 May 2006 and those who responded stressed the need for good links to the suburbs. In the west, it was proposed to prolong line T3 by about 2.5km to Porte d'Auteuil station (Métro line 10), but the exact course was not finalised and, following the municipal elections of 2008, this extension was deleted from the plans, as the area is already well served by public transport. The new mayor of that area preferred instead an extension of Métro line 9 in a loop and the placing of part of the RN10 main road in a tunnel, instead of "un tramway irréaliste" (an unrealistic tram line). Whether his ambitions were any more "réalistes" remains to be seen, since no steps have as yet been taken on either of these projects. The extension of the tram line appears to be still a possibility, being mentioned at the opening of the northern extension in December 2012, by Mme Anne Hidalgo, at that time principal assistant to the Mayor and a possible socialist candidate to follow him into office, as she duly did in 2014.

However, in the east and north much greater things were planned. Construction of an extension to Porte de Charenton, with interchange with Métro line 8, had already been agreed before the opening of the first section. With a view to gaining the Olympic Games of 2012, the city adopted a plan to extend the line from that point right round its eastern and north-eastern perimeter to Porte de la Chapelle (14.2km) in the north, thus recreating another large section of the Petite Ceinture railway, though not always following the exact course of the latter in the north-eastern area. This new section, with 26 stations, provides interchange with no fewer than eight Métro lines (plus branches 3bis and 7bis), while it passes close to line 14 at Porte de France. There is also interchange with 28 bus lines, as well as RER lines C and A and line E is not far away at Rosa Parks.[3]

The area served has a resident population of 170,000 living within 400m of the line and work opportunities for about 100,000 within the same distance. Even although Paris did not succeed in its

2 Système de Tramways à Efficacité Enérgetique Maximisé.

3 This station was originally to have been named Évangile and was referred to as such in the original plans.

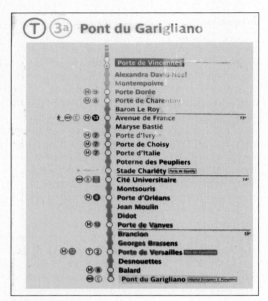

T3a Line diagram

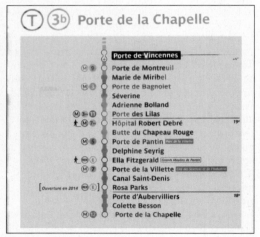

T3b Line diagram

Olympic ambitions, the city decided that it would still support the extension and a public enquiry began in May 2008, as a prelude to the granting of the DUP. A favourable report in autumn of that year allowed the scheme to go ahead and construction began early in 2009. Finance for the extension was agreed on 16 April 2009. In a side-swipe at President Sarkozy and

his ambitious plans for le Grand Paris, Mayor Delanoë, with the full support of M Jean-Paul Huchon, made it clear that this new tram line "montre la meilleure façon de faire en sorte que le Grand Paris répond aux besoins quotidiens des Franciliens" (shows the best way to make sure that le Grand Paris responds to the daily needs of the inhabitants of Île de France.)

The cost of the extension was expected to be €887 million (including rolling stock). Its length is 14.5km, and the final cost was €61.2 million/km.). Construction was managed by RATP in conjunction with Systra and the Mairie de Paris. Many schemes of urban improvement – the planting of trees, improvement of pavements and construction of cycle lanes – were carried out in connexion with the extension, at a cost €150.9 million, which was met by the City. This sum also included the commissioning of various works of art, it being the Mayor's expressed belief that "La beauté, l'art, la création ne sont pas reservés à une élite" (Beauty, art and creativity are not the preserve of an élite). Most of the line runs on grassed reservation, of 60,000 square metres of new turf, forming "Un tapis vert" (a green carpet), according to the Mayor.

The extension opened on Saturday 15 December 2012. There was no high-profile event, but MM Delanoë, Huchon and Mongin (Director of the RATP) were all present, along with local and regional politicians, and were welcomed by a large crowd of local people. Public service began in the afternoon and, as with the first opening of line T3, crowds turned out to sample the line and enthusiastic passengers often found that they had to wait for some time before being able to board a tram. Bus line PC2 and the eastern part of line PC3 were then withdrawn. It was expected that the extension would carry 165,000 passengers per day, on a peak hour headway of four minutes, taking the total number for what is now the 22.4km of line T3 to 300,000 per day. Average speed was intended to be 19/20km/hr – the buses of the PC lines managed (with some difficulty) 15.5km/hr, but it was not uncommon for a journey from Porte de la Chapelle to Porte de Vincennes to take almost an hour in the evening peak. The final cost of construction was €800 million, shared between the Region (€220 million) and the City of Paris. The rolling stock, whose cost was borne by the RATP, added a further €86 million.

The extension brought a change in the working of line T3, which was split into two lines, T3a and T3b,

meeting, but not with a common terminus, at Porte de Vincennes. Line T3a is an extension of the original line while T3b is entirely new construction. Unlike the first part of line T3, the extension has required several major construction works, which were largely responsible for the relatively high cost. At Porte de Vitry a flyover for road traffic had to be demolished to allow the passage of the tramway, while the parallel viaduct on the Petite Ceinture railway was replaced by a lighter bridge. To avoid two busy road intersections, the line then switches from central to side reservation, this change also permitting it to use the route of the former rail line across the Seine on the Pont National, although that bridge had to be widened to accommodate the new tracks. The line then continues to Porte de Vincennes, where it turns left to reach the terminal. A double track link across the road junction allows trams to run direct from one part of the line to the other but, at present, this is used only for special journeys.

The terminal arrangements at Porte de Vincennes are not ideal, as there are separate and parallel stations and passengers continuing their journey have to cross the busy cours de Vincennes. This choice was made to avoid blocking the rond-point de la Porte de Vincennes with trams and also to limit the effect of any delay on one part of the line. Passengers on the previous bus service did have to change where the bus crews took a lay-over, but this was simply a case of alighting and walking (or, more often, running) to the bus waiting immediately ahead. As standing passengers were first off and then found a seat, while those who had been seated now had to stand, all was quite fair in love and war on the PC bus. The transfer between trams is now rather more chaotic and in practice many of the younger and more agile passengers simply jump over the barriers and take their chance with the traffic, rather than wait at pedestrian crossing signals. It is also possible to use the access to the Métro station of line 1, to which new entrances have been provided but of course this involves negotiating steps and escalators.

The terminus of the northern section at Porte de Vincennes is placed immediately below the PC railway viaduct and on leaving it, trams run on a side reservation for a short distance before returning to a central reservation. From Porte de Montreuil northwards the line ceases to follow the course of the former railway, which at this point turned inwards towards the centre of the city. North of Porte de Pantin, it also forsakes the route of the bus line which it replaced, to allow better interchange with Métro line 7bis at Pré Saint-Gervais and also to serve the Hôpital Robert-Debré. It then rejoins the bus route and soon afterwards reaches the turning into the depot (see below). A new bridge had to be built to take it over the Canal de l'Ourcq, after which it runs next to SNCF main line tracks and reaches Ella Fitzgerald station[4], from which it is a short walk to Pantin SNCF station. There will also be interchange at Rosa Parks with the future extension of line T8 from Saint-Denis. Having made a detour to avoid a road tunnel, the line then arrives at Porte de la Villette, where it rejoins the former bus route, to continue to its present terminus just beyond the intersection at Porte de la Chapelle.

While trams working on the southern section of the extension share the existing depot, those running on the northern section – 25 in all – have their own depot and workshop located in Pantin, in an area at present in course of redevelopment. Clearly it was not easy to find a site of 38,000 square metres within a densely built urban area and the solution favoured was to adapt a site already belonging to the City, in this case the Ladoumegue stadium. Existing buildings on the site were adapted to house the trams on the ground floor. Work on the adaptation of these buildings began in January 2010 and was completed by the end of 2011, in time to house the first of the trams for the period of trial operation. Almost all the accommodation for the trams is under the roof of the existing building, apart from the workshop for routine maintenance and minor repairs, the offices and the control centre for the northern part of line T3, which are housed separately. Sufficient capacity has been built into the depot to allow it to house up to 50 additional trams in future, should extensions to the line require this. Much emphasis was placed on making the complex as environmentally-friendly as possible and photo-voltaic cells on the roof of the workshop provide heating while the washer uses stored rainwater, which after use is pumped into the adjacent Canal de l'Ourcq. The cost to the RATP was €90m but improvements, including a new gymnasium, the construction of 184 student residences and an upgrading of the embankments of the Canal required an additional €35m. The stadium closed at the end of the summer of 2011 and re-opened in rebuilt form in September 2013.

Work on the diversion of utilities began early in 2009 and was substantially complete by mid-2010. The Pont Masséna over the SNCF tracks to the south of Gare d'Austerliltz was widened at this time also, while on the Pont National, a new bridge for pedestrians had to be provided. To avoid the necessity to drive additional supports into the Seine, this was done by attaching a metal footbridge, designed by the architect Christian Devilliers, to the side of the existing structure. Twenty additional Citadis 402 trams were ordered in September 2010 to work the extension and work to prepare the trackbed also began at that date. At important intersections, such as that at Porte Dorée, prefabricated slabs, into which the rails had already been fitted, were used to minimise the construction time and thus delays to road traffic. The first rail was welded into place, in atrocious weather conditions, at la Villette on 24 January 2011, in a ceremony attended by the Mayor and M Mongin. The operation was supervised by Marine Brégeon who, at the age of 22, had already in 2009 been awarded a gold medal in welding at the Olympiades des Métiers (Craft Olympics). This extension creates extensive opportunities for the population of the eleven adjacent suburban communes which it serves. It is expected that 61% of all journeys made on it will have their origin or destination in a suburb.

Following a consultation exercise held in January and February 2011, the council of STIF agreed on 6 July of that year on a further extension of 4.3km and eight stations to Porte d'Asnières and the Batignolles area, which is to be the location of a new High Court building. The local mayor (in 2009) was in favour of this extension, as was Bertrand Delanoë in the 2008 campaign. The public enquiry for this section followed in January 2013, immediately after the extension to Porte de la Chapelle had been completed, and work began in 2014. It is hoped that this section will attract 76,000 passengers per day, as it will serve a local population of 186,000 and 90,000 work places. The cost is estimated at €193 million, plus €47 for the 14 additional trams which will be required. If all goes well, it is hoped to open this extension in December 2017. With the election of Mme Anne Hidalgo to the post of Mayor in 2014, it became likely that the line would be further prolonged to Porte Maillot and she also suggested, at a ceremony at Vincennes on 16 April of that year, that the entire Ceinture should be revived, though this could not be done before 2020. The Mayor of the 16th arrondissment, M Claude

Goasguen (UMP) immediately declared his total opposition to this idea, saying that trams will never enter the 16th. By its proponents it is thought that the presence of several sports centres such as the Stade Jean Bouin and the Parc des Princes, the new arts centre of the Fondation Louis Vuitton and the University Paris-Dauphine could generate sufficient traffic to make this extension viable.

Another possible extension mentioned in the electoral campaign of 2014 envisages a short line from cours de Vincennes to place de la Nation.

The extension is worked by 25 additional Citadis 402 trams of the same basic design as those already in use on line T3. The total cost of these was €86 million and the first was delivered to the depot at Porte de Pantin on 7 February 2012. Some internal modifications were made to the original design, mainly to improve access for passengers with reduced mobility, with facilities whose provision goes beyond that which is legally required. The trams have wider doorways, retractable plates to bridge the gap there and audio-visual announcements. Externally the cars carry the logo of STIF and its colours on a band above the windows.

References

Ville rail & Transports, 18 June 2008, 6 August 2008, 6 May 2009 (extension), 15 July 2009 (experiments on line T3), 10 February 2010 (Cour des comptes), 23 February 2011 (Pantin depot), 28 December 2011 (cargo trams), 21 February 2012 (first new tram), 16 May 2012 and 26 December 2012 (opening of extension), May 2014 (possible further extensions)

La Vie du Rail, 28 July 1999 (service via the Petite Ceinture)

Connaissance du Rail nos.340-341 (extension and STEEM system), 348-349 (STEEM)

Rail Passion no.168, October 2011 (work on extension)

Le Saga de la Petite Ceinture. Bruno Carrière. La Vie du Rail, Paris. Second edition 2001

Der Stadtverkehr 4/07

Publicity material issued by RATP.

4 This station was originally to be called Grands Moulins and was referred to as such in the original plans.

Line 3a

5.1. A train on the Petite Ceinture crosses the viaduct d'Auteuil in the years between 1900 and 1914. It is hauled by an 0-6-0 or 0-6-2 tank engine of class 3001, built by the Ch. de fer du Nord between 1876 and 1882 and therefore is most likely to be working from the Gare du Nord via the Ceinture back to that station. The train includes two guard's vans and the carriages are two-axle vehicles of the type used on the Ceinture from 1897 until its closure in 1934. The viaduct was built between 1864 and 1866 and demolished in 1958. The landing place of the bateaux mouches (river steamers) can be seen in the foreground and one of these is at the opposite bank. The medallions on the lower part of the bridge carry the letter N in honour of Napoléon III, who was instrumental in bringing the Ceinture into service.

PARIS — Viaduc d'Auteuil

5.2. Probably the last occasion on which the tracks of the Ceinture were used by passenger trains – though not in public service – occurred in 1997 when a short section near the former station of Maison Blanche was used for the trials of the MP89 stock destined for use on Métro line 14.

5.3. Place Balard station provides interchange with Métro line 8, whose terminus is located through the high bridge which once carried the trains of the Petite Ceinture. This view gives an indication of the problems of conversion which would have faced the authorities had they decided to use the trackbed of that line for the tramway. It might have been easier to take to the skies and travel by balloon.

5.4. The terminus of Pont de Garigliano is a two-platform station, to which access is obtained over a scissors crossover. Arriving tram no.305 waits until an outbound car clears the crossover on 19 September 2009.

5.5. Terminal arrangements here are not ideal and the passengers who had alighted from no.301 would have had to make their way across this unsignalled pedestrian crossing to connect with the PC1 bus.

5.6. Having safely negotiated the crossing, passengers hurry off to the waiting bus, 19 September 2009.

5.7. No.303 exchanges passengers at place Balard on 10 March 2007.

5.8. An evening scene at Porte de Versailles, with no.307 westbound on 3 May 2009. Trams of line T2 terminate to the south of this station, on the right in this view.

5.9. A view, looking towards Montrouge, of the arrangements at the actual gate of Porte d'Orléans, on a card posted in 1913. The fortifications can be seen on the right; when these were demolished the ground was used for the creation of a pleasant little park. In the centre is the gate for goods traffic, with a large cart passing through, and the collectors' offices, adorned with a plethora of notices. A variety of trams occupies the left hand side of the area. Lines TG and TAF of the CGO, both worked by compressed-air cars, terminated here, probably on the loop veering to the left, while the steam trams of the Paris-Arpajon radial line ran through the gate to Montrouge and beyond. The line from this point to Antony was electrified in 1901. One of the trailers is parked on the left and beyond it, steam tram engine no.15 and one of the electric trams can just be distinguished. Yet more variety was provided by the trams of the Cie des Tramways de la Rive gauche, whose line 2 reached the gate from the south, having come from Porte de Vincennes via Ivry. Central-entrance bogie cars were used and one is standing beside the eastern office building.

5.10. The new line runs about 100m north from the former scene. On 10 March 2007 no.324 approaches from the west. Here and at some other busy intersections, the station platforms are staggered on either side of the road junction, to leave more space for road traffic.

1472. MONTROUGE — La Porte d'Orléans   E. M.

5.11. Looking north from the site of the future station of Cité Universitaire on 4 November 2005.

5.12. The eastbound platform at this station in service on 10 March 2008.

5.13. The prettiest section on line T3a must be that at Potane des Peupliers. The evening sun strikes no.310, westbound, on 5 May 2013.

5.14. No.321 at Porte de Choisy on 10 March 2008. At present bus line 183 leaves from the right hand side of this platform and by 2019 new tram line T9 should occupy the same place.

5.15. The half-completed station at Porte d'Ivry in the rain on 25 June 2006.

5.16. The greenery had not as yet spread to the surroundings of avenue de France station, as of 1 May 2013. No.305 calls en route to Porte de Vincennes.

5.17. A view looking north at Porte Dorée in June 1980 when bus line PC was still operated as one service. Renault standard no.7902 is working on the "Intérieure" (inner) circle. The building on the right was originally the Colonial Museum and was built for the Colonial Exhibition of 1931, the last event for which much of the traffic was handled by trams. It now houses the Cité nationale de l'Histoire de l'immigration.

5.18. Works at the same intersection, looking north on 19 September 2011. To minimise disruption, the tracks in the centre had been laid in advance of that on the approach roads and that area then functioned as a roundabout.

5.19. The scene on 1 May 2013, with the works completed and the tracks and trees in place.No.303 approaches the southbound platform. There has been a marked reduction in road traffic since 1980.

5.20. The intersection, looking south along the boulevard Poniatowski on 4 June 2011. Renault Agora articulated no.4549, on line PC2, gives its passengers a bumpy ride over the temporary road surface.

5.21. Not quite two years later, on 1 May 2013, everything is tidy, motor traffic has been reduced and public transport, in the shape of no.316, has precedence at the crossroads.

5.22. An attractive mural at Porte Dorée northbound platform. "Golden flowers bloom along the boulevard des Maréchaux".

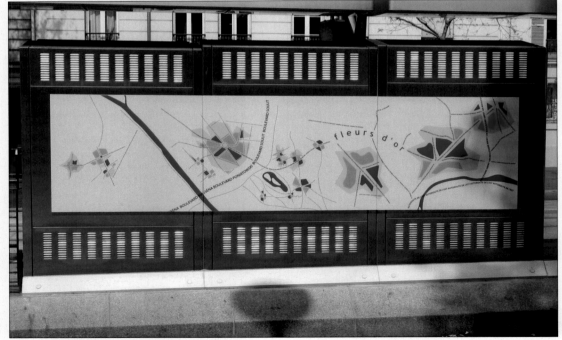

147. PARIS — Cours de Vincennes. Station du Métro et du Tramway

5.23. The terminus of the Chemins de fer Nogentais at Porte de Vincennes c1905. Two of the company's 54-seat double-deckers of 1900, nos. 8 and 48 are present and the former, with an open cross-bench trailer in tow, is about to set off for the rural delights of Noisy-le-Grand. On the right is part of the Guimard pavilion which marks the entrance to the terminus of Métro line 1.

5.24. On 28 September 2011 works have begun to lay the new terminal siding for line T3a. As yet no alterations have been made to the entrance to the station of line 1, still marked by its Dervaux candelabra. The station was rebuilt in 1937, after line 1 had been extended to Château de Vincennes and the pavilion was, regrettably, removed.

5.25. By 4 July 2012 the trackwork is complete and the entrance has again been totally rebuilt, with a new style of canopy and an escalator for passengers leaving the station.

5.26. The terminus in service on 1 May 2013. Having reversed, no.316 moves forward to deal with the waiting crowd.

5.27. Not everyone will find a seat. This view was taken at an off-peak time – at rush hours it is difficult to see the tram for the passengers. The bridge over the roof of no.316 formerly carried the Petite Ceinture over the cours de Vincennes.

5.28. A view of the capacious interior of one of the Citadis trams of lines T3a and b.

5.29. The lighting scheme at the stations is attractive. A scene at Porte d'Orléans.

Line 3b

5.30. On 4 July 2012 work was progressing on the north side station at Porte de Vincennes.

5.31. The station in service on 18 March 2015, with a lunch-time crowd preparing to board no.336.

5.32. Looking north to the junction from the south side of the cours de Vincennes in May 2011. The track bed has been made ready and road traffic diverted but as yet there is no sign of rails or overhead.

5.33. Just over one year later, on 4 July 2012, rails and overhead are in position north of the junction and all that remains to be done is to tidy up the site.

5.34. The line in service on 1 May 2013. No.345 prepares to turn in to the terminal siding.

5.35. A grey morning at Porte de Montreuil on 21 September 2014, as no.334 calls northbound. At least there is some greenery, courtesy of line T3b, to brighten up the view beyond the intersection. The entrance to the Métro station on line 9 is on the right at the traffic lights.

5.36. The station at Hôpital Robert Debré brings a good deal of traffic to the trams. On 18 September 2015 no.328 is bound for Porte de Vincennes.

5.37. The complex road junction at Porte de Pantin was formerly a black spot for the buses working on the PC service and it was not unknown for a driver to have to spend up to 20 minutes coaxing his vehicle through the competing streams of traffic. Traffic is still heavy and noisy but thanks to their dedicated right-of-way and priority at signals, the trams have few problems. No.410 is passing below the viaduct of the boulevard Péripherique on 3 May 2013.

5.38. The station at Porte de la Villette has passenger shelters of an unusual design and there is cross-platform interchange with numerous bus lines. No.332 runs into the platform for southbound passengers on 29 May 2015.

5.39. Beyond la Villette, trams cross the Canal de Saint-Denis and two pass each other on the handsome bridge. On the Canal, a (free) frequent service is provided by solar-powered catamarans from this point to le Millénaire, a large shopping centre, and one of the vessels, named after the centre, manoeuvres into the landing stage on its return journey. The trams are not the sole environmentally-friendly form of transport in this area.

5.40. The line then turns to pass under the mainline out of Gare de l'Est, on which a train made up of new Transilien suburban stock is seen while no. 346 runs down to pass under the tracks.

5.41. There may be an absence of greenery at Porte de la Villette but there is certainly plenty at the next station, Canal de Saint-Denis.

5.42. An interesting piece of artwork on the passenger shelter at this station, play on words connected with the tramway.

(Illustrations nos.39-42 were taken on 29 May 2015)

5.43. Rosa Parks will from December 2015 provide interchange between the trams and RER line and other suburban trains from Gare de l'Est to the eastern suburbs. On 1 May 2013 an eye-catching notice tells of the facilities to come.

5.44. The number of cranes surrounding the tram station (on the same day) gives an idea of the amount of building work going on in this area. Both housing and office blocks are under construction, as no.327 approaches, bound for Porte de la Chapelle, 1 May 2013.

5.45. By 29 May 2015 most of the buildings are ready for occupation and their distinctive design is evident. No.342 is at the station.

5.46. Excavations on the boulevard Ney on 19 September 2009.

5.47. With the diversion of utilities completed, work could start on the preparation of the track bed. A view looking west, at approximately the same spot as the previous illustration, and through traffic can resume. Bus no.1811 was on line PC2 on 4 June 2011.

5.48. Track laying and construction of a pedestrian area require further diversions. Bus no.1854 on 4 July 2012.

5.49. The final result. On 3 May 2013 tram no.345 has just left Colette Besson station.

5.50. The present northern terminus of the line is at Porte de la Chapelle, where the station was under construction on 4 July 2012.

5.51. During this period, the usual problems of traffic at this junction were greatly increased by diversions and the buses of line PC2 had to use a temporary stop.

5.52. As opened, there is cross-platform interchange between the trams which terminate here and the buses on line PC3 which take passengers onwards for all stops to Pont de Garigliano. No.313 has just arrived on 1 May 2013.

5.53. At the time of writing, work is progressing on the further extension to Porte d'Asnières and on 29 May 2015 a notice at Porte de Clichy explains about the diversion and modernisation of utilities.

5.54. Slightly to the east, at Lycée Honoré de Balzac, traffic is confined to a single lane in each direction while work continues on the future central reservation for the trams. Sometimes this has disastrous consequences for the bus services, but in this view modern MAN single-decker no.9903 is not in passenger service.

Chapter 6
Line T4 « La Ligne des Coquetiers »

Yet another variation in tramway operation is provided by line T4.

This line of 8km running between Bondy and Aulnay-sous-Bois in the north-eastern suburbs also replaces a railway service, of which the first section opened for traffic in 1875. It was jointly owned by the Chemin de fer de l'Est (Bondy – Gargan) and the Chemin de fer du Nord (Aulnay – Gargan) and passed to the SNCF in January 1938. Its name of "La Ligne des Coquetiers" (the Eggcup Line) recalls the agricultural nature of the area when it was built. It was worked more as a tramway than a railway line and as urban growth reached out to the area it served, it became virtually a tramway on reserved track in the middle of leafy suburban streets. A large number of level crossings, 14 in all, hindered operation and, given the frequent closures, caused considerable problems for motorists. Queues of cars developed and at times these had not totally cleared after one train before the barriers came down for the next. The southern section from Bondy to Gargan was electrified at 25kV AC in May 1962 but the portion from that point to Aulnay was not converted until September 1977. Latterly the line was worked by electric locomotives of class BB16500 and sets of stainless steel suburban stock, working in push-pull mode. As the northern part remained single track, headways could not be more than one train every 30 minutes beyond Gargan and passenger numbers declined to 9,600 per day by 2000. The fall in traffic was particularly marked after the cessation of through services to Gare de l'Est on the opening of RER line E in 1999. Bondy and Gargan had also at one time been served by trams running through from central Paris on the lines of the Est Parisien company.

After consideration of various options, it was decided in 2000, mainly on grounds of cost, to replace the trains by tram-trains. This option would allow the reuse of much of the existing infrastructure. The line would be upgraded, not only to improve transport facilities in the immediate area, but also to serve as a test track for the future widespread introduction of tram-trains in other parts of France. Future extensions could be made as street tramways. The SNCF service ended on 14 December 2003.

The northern section was given double track, necessitating the construction of a new viaduct over the main RN3 road at Gargan. A new bridge was also constructed over the Canal de l'Ourcq. The level crossings were converted to normal road intersections with colour light signalling and three new halts were built, at Remise à Joelle, Lycée Henri Seller and Rougemont-Chanteloup . To keep costs down, much track was reused, as well as many of the overhead fittings. The line was changed to right-hand running and, together with altered clearances, it is now not possible for main-line trains to use it. Railway signalling was totally replaced by tramway-type signalling, although the trams are equipped to work with railway signalling when running on the main line. Drivers, many of whom were recruited through a scheme run by the Département, had to undergo a course of instruction lasting one year before being passed to work on the new line. A new control centre was constructed at Gargan. Stations were rebuilt and in all but two cases the original station buildings were demolished, against the wishes of the local authorities. The opportunity was taken to make Bondy station fully accessible. At 2001 prices, the rebuilding of the infrastructure cost €52.72 million, of which 47% was met by the Région, 23.5% by central government, 18.5% by RFF, 9.3% by the Département of Seine – St-Denis and the balance of 1.8% by SNCF.

The line was formally re-opened on 18 November 2006 by Mme A-M Idrac, President of SNCF, and M J-P Huchon. The opening ceremony was somewhat marred by brake problems with two of the new cars, leading to a temporary suspension of service. Commercial service began two days later. Service has been much improved to give a frequency of six minutes at peak times and of nine minutes at other times and this encouraged a growth in passenger numbers to 40,000 per day by 2012. Given the short length of the line (7.9km), a passenger count in the region of 14 million per annum speaks volumes for the success of the tram-trains. Initially, over-enthusiastic use of the loud air horns at every road crossing caused much annoyance to local people. These were subsequently toned down by 15 db and later the SNCF regulations were altered to require use of these horns only in emergencies.

Some criticisms of the conversion can be made. Although the stations are adequate, no attempt was made to design these to the standard adopted by RATP. The use of ballasted rather than grassed track divides one side of the street from the other and still maintains some of the railway atmosphere. There might have been even more new passengers had the service been prolonged inwards to Noisy-le-Sec to provide interchange with lines T2 and, in future, M15. Nonetheless the conversion has been a considerable achievement.

Since the line required a maximum of ten tram-trains for service, there was a surplus of rolling stock and on 4 July 2011 the 10km branch line running between Esbly and Crécy-la-Chapelle, in the outer north-eastern suburbs, was converted to tram-train operation. A new timetable was implemented on 3 September, offering a half-hourly frequency in peak periods and an hourly frequency at other times, with the last services now running at 22.30. The branch is electrified at 25kV AC throughout and thus there is no need for a change of voltage. The tram-trains replaced rakes of RIB/RIO stainless steel stock of some vintage, hauled by locomotives of class BB17000 and the comfort of the new vehicles was much appreciated by passengers. The reduction in running costs was no doubt equally appreciated by managers.

Rolling Stock

Line T4 remains in the hands of SNCF and is now worked by 15 Siemens Avanto five-section tram-trains, following the award of a contract on 28 June 2002. The total cost of the rolling stock, €68 million, was met by SNCF. Twelve cars of the same type were ordered for use at Mulhouse but an option for a further 20 was not taken up. These are the first tram-trains to run in France, the first low floor tram-trains and, at present, the only trams anywhere to use 25kV AC. They are dual-voltage but at present the facility to change to 750V DC is not used. Maximum speed is 100km/hr but this is attained only when running on the mainline to and from the depot. On line T4 the maximum is 70km/hr, but this is seldom attained, due to the short inter-station distances and the need to slow down for road crossings. These trams carry two fleet numbers, one being an SNCF rolling stock number and the other a simple fleet number, prefixed by the letters TT (TT01-15). Within each tram each section has its own SNCF carriage number; thus in TT01 the numbers run 25501 25101 25201 25301 25502. Clearly these fine trams might be considered extravagant for a short line of this nature, but there are plans for extensions and the operator no doubt wished to gain experience of running this type of car before embarking on schemes elsewhere in France. The trams are shedded and maintained at the mainline depot at Noisy-le-Sec.

Technical details

Length 36.36m, width 2.65m, 4 x 130kW motors, 242 passengers, 80 seated.

Extension

The area to the east of the line, centred on Clichy-sous-Bois, has in recent years seen many social problems, culminating in rioting in 2005 which caused damage to the value of €220 million. One of the causes of this was considered to be the high rate of unemployment, especially among young people (23%), and it was clearly essential to improve transport in the area to allow the inhabitants access to a much wider range of opportunities. The Communes of Clichy-sous-Bois and of Montfermeil prepared plans, with a budget of €600 million to improve the area and attract residents who would be able to contribute more to local taxation. One part of the programme centred on an extension of line T4 by 6.5km to Livry-Gargan, Clichy-sous-Bois and Montfermeil. These plans stalled for some time, due to opposition from local politicians in Livry-Gargan and Pavillons-sous-Bois, who feared the impact of tram-trains on narrow roads in the area. However the promise of a busway, with a high quality service, along the line of the RN3 road removed these fears and allowed the scheme to go ahead. The public enquiry recommended that particular attention should be paid to traffic considerations at Gargan.

The junction with the existing line will be at Gargan, laid out to allow a service from Bondy to Montfermeil. From Gargan station, the line will run on grassed reserved track along the boulevard de la République and turn sharp left then right to serve

6.1. The line diagram for lines T4 and the branch from Esbly to Crécy-la-Chapelle.

two stations in Clichy-sous-Bois. Two more right-angled turns will bring it to Clichy-Montfermeil and it will terminate at the central hospital. Interchange with the future Métro line 17 will be possible at this point in 2024. The branch will have a total of 11 stations. The DUP for the extension was approved in September 2013 and work began in 2014, with an estimated opening date of 2017. A daily passenger count of 37,000 is anticipated and the basic frequency will be six minutes. The infrastructure cost is expected to be €260 million, as it will be necessary to build a depot for the extended line. Some of the funding was earmarked under the Plan de Relance de l'Économie.

A total of 14 tram-trains will be required to serve the existing line and the extension, these being financed by STIF, at an estimated cost of €60 million. It is likely that these will come from the order for Citadis Dualis vehicles, with the existing fleet being transferred to serve on provincial lines. On the extension, cars will use 750V DC.

References

Der Stadtverkehr 06/05 (rolling stock), 1-2/07 (opening)

To-day's Railways Europe no.168

La Vie du Rail, 14 September 2011. (Crécy branch).

6.2. Cross-platform interchange at Bondy in July 2000. Passengers who have alighted from one of the new M12N trains on RER line E cross to the Aulnay train, made up of a locomotive-hauled set of three RIB (Rame Inoxydable de Banlieue) two-coach units.

6.3. Interchange on 10 March 2007. With two tracks and platforms, the terminus of tram-trains of line T4 is rather more spacious than the former arrangement. The MI2N set is bound for Chelles and no.01 waits to set off for Aulnay-sous-Bois.

6.4. A closer view of no.01.

6.5. The first station from Bondy is Remise à Joelle. No.05 approaches on 10 March 2007.

6.6. The line then turns away from the mainline tracks. Electric locomotive no.16580 approaches les Coquetiers in July 2000.

6.7. Running on the right, no.08 approaches les Coquetiers on 21 March 2015. The former station building, restored but not currently in use, is on the left.

6.8. Homeward-bound commuters stream from a six-car train of VIB stock at les Coquetiers on a sunny evening in July 2000.

6.9. The rule of the road has been changed and tram-trains run on the right, while commodious shelters, complete with modern ticket machines, have been provided on the platforms. Otherwise little has changed at les Coquetiers as no.08 calls on 21 March 2015.

6.10. A view of Gargan station on the same date, with no.11 bound for Aulnay.

6.11. The level crossing at the north end of Gargan station in July 2000. The barriers have come down to allow a train bound for Bondy to leave the single track and cross the road on the approach to the station.

6.12. The level crossing is now controlled by road traffic lights and the "petit cordonnier" (little cobbler) has had to move to make way for the re-arrangement and doubling of the tracks. However, Renault is still in business. No.03 runs into the station on 10 March 2007. The tracks of the extension to Clichy-sous-Bois will go off to the right at this point.

6.13. A tram-train crosses the bridge over the canal de l'Ourcq.

6.14. The cars may not reach their full potential on this line, but they certainly attain high speeds on the longer inter-station sections. No.12 must have been doing at least 50km/hr on the slight gradient leading up to the bridge when seen on the same day.

6.15. At level crossings, the red phase for road traffic is very brief, of the order of 30 seconds. Cars are still crossing as no.10, running at a fair speed, is within a few metres of the crossing at the south end of Rougemount station.

6.16. Finally, a few seconds later, the lights have gone to red for road traffic and the tram-train has priority.

6.17. Rougemont-Chanteloup is one of the new halts built for the tram-trains. No.03 approaches while in the background a northbound train of RER line B leaves Aulnay.

6.18. No.11 in the terminal tracks at Aulnay-sous-Bois on 21 March 2015.

6.19. An interior view of no.11.

(Nos.12-19 were taken on 21 March 2015.)

Chapter 7
Line T5 Saint-Denis – Garges-Sarcelles
« Le tram avance – la Ville change »

Plans to improve transport in this corridor were drawn up in 1994, envisaging the construction of a busway as far as Sarcelles, but these were not implemented. However, a further study recommended that this line should be incorporated in the plans for the contract between the Région and central government covering the years 2000-2006. However it was not until 2003 that a more detailed study was undertaken, leading to a public enquiry and to the granting of the DUP in 2005 and approval by the STIF in the following year. This line runs between Saint-Denis and Garges-Sarcelles, a distance of 6.6km. At one time, the part of this route as far as Pierrefitte was served by trams of lines 11b and 65, on a single line reserved track, running through to Porte de Clignancourt and place de la République, but these were replaced by buses in 1936. Line T5 is therefore the first of the new lines to follow the course of a former tram line for any distance. For much of its length it is on the main road which was formerly the RN1, now RD301, and traverses the areas of two Départements, Seine-Saint-Denis and Val d'Oise, serving densely populated suburbs, which have suffered from equally dense motor traffic.

In 2007 it was decided by RATP to construct the line as a "tramway à pneus" (rubber-tyred tramway), on the Lohr system rather than as a busway or a conventional tramway. The reason given for this choice was that this could provide a service approaching that of a tramway while allowing easy insertion of the line into an already heavily built-up area, with some narrow roads. The platform of the line is 20% narrower than that required for a conventional double-track tramway and this has allowed the retention of two traffic lanes on the roadway on each side of the line. It was also constructed with less excavation for the track foundations, thus keeping down the cost, an important factor for a line which was then expected to attract a ridership of only 30,000 passengers per day. The wisdom of adopting a different form of technology for an area which is already served by trams may be questioned and in practice it is only too easy for road vehicles to stray onto the tracks, with consequent disruption of the service.

The cost of the entire line, including rolling stock, was €228 million, about €34.5million/km. The infrastructure cost of €163.13 was shared between the Région (71.5%), the French government (17%), the Département of Val d'Oise (10%) and the RATP (1.5%) The cost of the trams was met by STIF. The first rails were laid on 30 June 2010 and by mid-2011 work was well advanced. The line was formally opened on 29 July 2013, with free rides being given to the public on 3 and 4 August. The line is 6.6km long and has 16 stations.

From its terminus at Marché de Saint-Denis, line T5 runs due north for three kilometres, serving the suburbs of Saint-Denis, the University of Paris VIII, a branch of the National Archives of France at Stade Delaune and a new urban development on one of the last areas of agricultural land in the district. It then reaches the suburb of Pierrefitte-sur-Seine, a commune of 28,000 people which is still growing rapidly. Much of this growth is along the line of the former RN1 and as a result almost all the population lives within 500m of a station. The depot is located at Pierrefitte. The line at this point passes under the course of the future Tram-Express-Nord, then veers slightly to the east on to RN16 to reach Sarcelles, where it turns sharply to the south-east to serve that Commune, of 58,000 inhabitants and the most cosmopolitan in the Paris area. It includes three high-rise blocks of flats dating from the period 1955-75, now the subject of much criticism as a form of urban development. From there it continues to the terminus at Garges-Sarcelles station, situated on RER line D. There is easy interchange with tramline T1 at Saint-Denis, but of course there is no possibility of through running. Two bridges over railway lines on the course of the line had to be rebuilt, while at Pierrefitte that over the outer ring road had to be demolished and totally rebuilt. Including the termini, there are 16 stations. The construction of the line was accompanied by a certain amount of environmental improvement and the planting of a large number of trees along its course, under the direction of the landscape artist Jean-Marc l'Anton. The few surviving large planes were replaced by smaller trees and lines of bushes and shrubs of varied perfume were planted between the main highway and the cycle lanes and pedestrian spaces, to shield these from the still-dense traffic.

Already by the end of 2014, the line was clearly becoming a victim of its own success. Intended to transport 35,000 passengers per day, it was carrying 50,000 and the total was still increasing.

Rolling stock

Line T5 is worked by 15 double-ended three-section STE3 cars, built by Lohr Industrie and numbered 501-515. These are 25m long and 2.2m wide. The height is only 2.89m and when the cars are crowded, as they are for most of the day, they are very, very crowded and the interior is distinctly claustrophobic. The financial problems which that firm faced during the period of their construction delayed the opening of the line by seven months from the original date of December 2012. With a capacity of 178 passengers, lower than most modern trams in France, these nevertheless cost €3.47 million per vehicle, giving a total cost of €52 million. Average speed is 18km/hr, with a frequency of a tram every five minutes. Acceleration is impressive, but riding qualities are less commendable – the motion can only be described as "wobbly" when running at any speed; it gives the impression that the concrete on which the car is running has not quite set. To meet the needs of increasing traffic, three or five additional cars may be ordered.

It will be interesting to see if the decision to introduce this new form of transport in the Paris area is justified by the performance and cost of operation of these "tramways à pneus". Line T5 is already a busy service and it is not clear what would happen should passenger numbers outgrow the capacity of the system.

References

Connaissance du Rail, nos.348-349 April – May 2010

Ville rail &Transports 3 September 2013.

7.1. Line diagram.

7.2. Publicity for the new line at Marché de Saint-Denis in June 2012.

7.3. Another poster explains how the new tramway will help the local environment.

7.4. Opening day publicity at Pierrefitte.

7.5. Publicity at Saint-Denis on 6 June 2012.

7.6. The almost-completed terminus at Saint-Denis on the same day.

7.7. The station in service on 25 September 2013, with a crowd of passengers waiting to board no.509

7.8. With some evidence of new planting in the foreground, no.513 crosses to the down line as it approaches the terminus. As it is impossible to have a scissors crossover on a Translohr line, there are separate down and up crossovers here.

7.9. With the works at the new station of Alcide d'Obigny in the background, bus no.2463 pulls away from a stop in Pierrefitte on the evening of 29 June 2012.

7.10. The same location, fifteen months later, with the tram station in service.

7.11. The Hôtel de Ville of Pierrefitte is an attractive building of the 1930s. Through traffic clearly remains a problem at this point, as an inbound tram pauses at the station, 25 September 2013.

7.12. The Commune of Sarcelles experienced a meteoric growth, from 8,300 inhabitants in 1954 to 52,000 in 1968, with a continued, though slower rise, to 60,000 to-day. Many of the new inhabitants live in high rise blocks and the centre of the town is dominated by the towers of the commercial centre of Les Flanades; this attracts shoppers from a wide area. Tram no.512 approaches, bound for the outer terminus on 25 September 2013.

7.13. The terminal station of Garge-Sarcelles provides interchange with line D of the RER. No.509 draws into the station while another tram reverses on the crossover beyond.

7.14. A general view of one of the cars, no.514 at les Flanades.

7.15. An interior view of no.513.

Chapter 8
Line T6 « Avec le Tram – plus proche, plus vert »

Originally intended as an extension of line 13 of the Métro, then as a separate, automatic métro, this line was finally built as another "tram à pneus". Although the RATP itself was not entirely happy with the decision, it was made on the grounds of the supposed silence of operation (though in practice there is little to choose between the rubber-tyred cars and conventional trams) and on the undoubted hill-climbing and curve-taking abilities of the system. Other reasons for the choice included the rather questionable one of fire risk in a tunnel section. The project was first outlined in 2000 but it was not until 9 February 2006 that the DUP was issued. Considerable difficulties then arose from the presence of former quarry workings and the need to put the final section from Vélizy to the western terminus into tunnel under the Forest of Meudon and these considerably retarded the start of construction. Work finally began late in 2011 and the excavation of the tunnel began in the spring of 2012. Construction from Châtillon as far as Vélizy was well advanced by the summer of 2013. Trials of the rolling stock were started in the summer of 2014, followed by the "marche à blanc" on 8 November 2014 and, after a formal presentation on 1 December, the line opened for service on 13 December, from Châtillon-Montrouge to Robert Wagner. The remainder of the line will open in 2016.

The final cost of the line, excluding rolling stock, is estimated to be €384.08 million, €27.42 million/km, of which half was met by the Région, 20% by Hauts-de-Seine, 16% by central government, 13% by Yvelines and the balance of 1% by RATP.

Line T6 runs for 14km in a wide arc across the relatively affluent suburbs of the south-west, many of which were developed between the two world wars. There are 21 stations and it is expected that 90,000 passengers per day will use this line when it has been completed. It begins in the centre of the Commune of Châtillon, at an excellent interchange with Métro line 13 and many local bus lines and, having gained the main shopping street, avenue de Paris, runs in an almost-straight line in a south-westerly direction through the western part of that commune, with five stations. Between Parc André Malraux and Division Leclerc the line climbs steadily for over 1km on the avenue de Verdun, to reach the commune of Clamart, in which there are six stations. The large Hôpital Béclère is likely to account for much of the traffic on this section. At Pavé Blanc station the line turns due north and passes along the narrow street of the same name, on which motor traffic is controlled by signals to give priority to the trams. Having reached the large modern estate, Georges Pompidou, served by the station of that name, the line again makes a sharp turn, this time to the left, to serve the Commune of Meudon-la-Forêt, which for long has suffered from poor transport links with the surrounding areas and has thus been something of a backwater. One of the main aims of the planners of line T6 is to end this isolation. It then arrives at Vélizy 2, which serves a large commercial centre built in 1968, when it was intended that the private car would provide the main form of transport. The new line should alter this situation and a large interchange has been developed at the entrance to the centre. From there line T6 runs through a new commercial area to Robert Wagner. In 2016 the extension to Viroflay Rive Droite will be opened, most of this being in tunnel under the Forest of Meudon, with one intermediate station at Viroflay Rive Gauche. Both of these stations will afford excellent interchange with the suburban lines from Montparnasse and Saint-Lazare to Versailles and, in the case of the latter, RER line C.

Trials of rolling stock began in February 2014, the training of drivers followed in April and the line between Châtillon-Montrouge and Robert Wagner was brought into service on 13 December 2014.

Depot and workshops

These facilities are located at Vélizy-Villacoublay, in an area not previously well served by public transport, though that has changed with the opening of T6. The complex has been built to the south of the A86 motorway, while the line proper is to the north of this and an underpass takes trams from or to the depot. In the workshops, four roads are devoted to the maintenance of the vehicles, of which three have facilities to allow the cars to be lifted and two have walkways to give access to the equipment mounted on their roofs. The exterior of the building is clad in wood, to emphasise its environmentally-friendly nature and this impression is reinforced by such facilities as LED lighting, storage of rain water and recycling of the water used for washing the trams. Outside there are two storage roads, one of which is equipped to carry out light repairs and maintenance, while access to the second, which is enclosed, is through the washing machine. The sidings, situated to the north of the building, have room for up to 32 cars and the depot also houses the control centre, an administrative area and the offices for the crews.

Rolling Stock

The line is worked by 28 cars, numbered 601-628, of the STE6 design of Translohr. This is the first line to use such cars, the total length of 46m being necessary to give a capacity more or less equal to that of a conventional tramway and these are in fact the longest trams in France. The width is 2.20m, as in other examples of Translohr cars. The capacity is 252 passengers, of whom 60 are seated. To cope with the gradients of line T6, the trams have been fitted with two additional motors, each mounted on one of the wheels of the intermediate axles. The interior décor is based on slate-grey, relieved by a shade of "anis" (yellow-green) and turquoise on the seats and the side panels, while the seats have a floral pattern in grey. Ordered in September 2010, these cars were built while Translohr was going through a period of crisis and there was all-round relief that construction went ahead more or less on schedule and the first tram (no.602) was shown at the opening of the depot and maintenance complex at Vélizy-Villacoublay on 14 October 2013. The cost of this fleet, funded by STIF, was €137 million, €4.89 million per car. Compared to the cost of a conventional tram of equivalent capacity, this is a high figure.

References

Ville rail & Transports 29 October 2013 (depot and rolling stock), April 2014 (trials), January 2015 (choice of Translohr)

Der Stadtverkehr. 5/15.

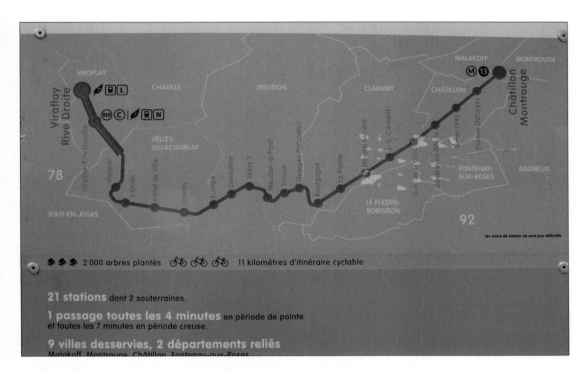

8.1. A map of the line displayed at Châtillon in May 2013.

8.2. The length of the six-section cars is stressed in this view of no.622 in the temporary terminal siding at Robert Wagner on 22 March 2015.

8.3. An interior view of one of the cars. The décor is attractive, but it cannot completely banish the impression of sitting in a very long and narrow tube.

8.4. The terminus at Châtillon, located under a new office block, provides easy interchange with line 13 of the Métro, which is here above ground level on an embankment. In the early evening of 22 March 2015 passengers for the trains leave by the far end of the station, while no.618 prepares to run out to the siding where it will reverse for its next journey.

8.5. Works in the avenue de Paris in Châtillon on 3 May 2013 have squeezed motor traffic to the two lanes on the right in this view.

8.6. By March 2015 all is in order again and no.630 has a clear run on its approach to the terminus. Road traffic is still confined to the two lanes on the right, but with rather more space than in the previous view. The side road on the left is for access only.

8.7. The works made life difficult for bus drivers and passengers, as illustrated by this view taken near the present station of Vauban on 3 May 2013. Renault Agora no.2801 bound for Porte d'Orléans on line 194 picks up passengers from a temporary stop on the trackbed of the future line and a pedestrian uses it as a short cut.

8.8. Vauban station on 22 March 2015. No.616 is inbound.

8.9. From the western edge of Châtillon trams climb the long gradient of the avenue de Verdun to reach Division Leclerc, the first station in Clamart.

8.10. Publicity for the new service and the new station, seen on 5 May 2013.

8.11. The station in service on 22 March 2015.

8.12-8.15. Tracklaying on a Translohr system is rather different to that on a conventional tramway, as illustrated by these views taken near Soleil Levant. The road surface is first excavated in the normal manner, but to a lesser depth than on a conventional tramway, and the trackbed is covered with concrete, with a channel left clear for the central rail. (12). Rails are then brought to the site (13) and placed in these channels (14). Finally the concrete is poured, the stations are completed and service can begin (15). This last view, taken on 22 March 2015, also gives an idea of the housing development which has followed the new line, clearly at the expense of the attractive little chalet-style houses seen in the previous view and this one.

8.13

8.14

8.15.

8.16. The route de Pavé Blanc still retains something of the atmosphere of a village street and this has required the use of signals to allow trams and traffic to share the restricted space. No.622 is bound for Vélizy on 22 March 2015.

8.17. Works at the future station Georges Pompidou, looking north, on 5 May 2013.

8.18. The same view, with no.620 approaching the completed station on 22 March 2015.

8.19. A view of the station on the same day, with no.616 bound for Vélizy. Interchange with several bus lines is provided here.

8.20. As the roadway at the next station, Georges Millandy, is of restricted width, an island platform is used. To separate conflicting flows of passengers, westbound trams stop at the eastern end of the long platform and eastbound trams use the western end.

8.21. Vélizy is clearly an area in course of rapid development. A view looking west from the future station of Vélizy 2 on 6 May 2013.

8.22. No.602 in the completed station on 22 March 2015.

8.23. The commercial development continues to the west of Vélizy. No.607 is on trial at Dewoitine on 11 July 2014.

8.24. Until the tunnel section to Viroflay was completed, trams terminated at Robert Wagner, where no.616 is seen on the same date.

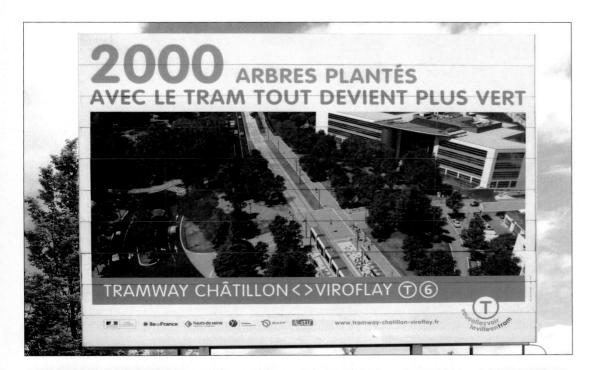

8.25. Before the line opened, posters stressed its green credentials.

8.26. A view looking north from Robert Wagner, showing the line under construction in the Forest of Meudon in March 2015. It disappears into the tunnel section after taking the curve to the left.

Chapter 9
Line T7. « Tram 7– toutes les cinq Minutes »

Most of this line lies on the course of the road which was formerly designated RN7 (trunk road 7), but has recently been reclassified RD7. This road leads due south from Paris to the once-royal town of Fontainebleau and on to Lyon, Marseille and the Mediterranean. In 1955 Charles Trenet (1913-2001) wrote the song "Route Nationale 7" as "Une route qui fait recette" (a road which brings in the money) and from the 1930s onwards the money was earned by consecrating the surrounding area almost entirely to meet the needs of the motor vehicle and its occupants, many of whom would be enjoying their first holidays with pay. Until recently it was not noted for the quality of its architecture, with numerous garages, car showrooms, fast food outlets and other similar signs of the motor era. However, the environment is changing rapidly; much new housing will be constructed here in the near future and there is also substantial commercial development in the area.

This line was envisaged originally as an extension of a Métro line (7) but the proposal was changed to become one for a conventional tramway running from Villejuif –Louis-Aragon station on the southern branch of that line, southwards for a distance of 11.2km to Athis-Mons, with a later extension to Juvisy-sur-Orge. The main reason for the construction of the line was to improve public transport links to serve Orly airport's freight terminal and the new central market at Rungis, opened in 1961 and 1969 respectively to become the largest combined centre of employment in the southern part of Île-de-France but unfortunately developed without much regard for local public transport. There was also a pressing need to provide a more suitable feeder to the Métro than the chronically-overcrowded buses of lines 185 and 285, successors to tram service 85 of former days, which ran from Châtelet to Villejuif. Southbound buses were often almost full when they arrived at Villejuif from the inner suburbs, to the annoyance of passengers changing from the Métro. Construction of the line also made it possible to rehabilitate the area immediately surrounding the RD7 and to improve the general environment. Chronologically the line should have been numbered T6 but as it mainly runs along the road numbered RD7 and also feeds into Métro line 7, it was logical to give it the designation of T7.

The line serves the Départements of Val de Marne and Essonne.

Preliminary studies were undertaken in the winter of 2000/2001 and the scheme was approved in principle by the council of STIF in October 2002. A public enquiry followed between December 2003 and February 2004 and the DUP, which had to be approved by the Prefects of the two Départements, was issued exactly one year later, on 1 February 2005. Detailed plans were prepared in 2006 but these were then subject to modifications and it was not until October 2008 that they were finally approved. Work on the alterations to the RD7 began in December 2008 and the first rail was welded at Rungis on 29 June 2011. Trial running of the new trams began in July 2013 and the line was finally opened for traffic, slightly early, on 16 November 2013. Bus line 185 was then withdrawn south of Villejuif and diverted to Choisy, while line 285 was cut back to Athis-Mons, where, for the time being, it provides an onward connexion to Juvisy. Eighteen other bus lines were modified to provide better interchange with the trams. The end-to-end running time is 33 minutes, giving an average speed of 20.36km/hr. It is expected that it will be used by 28,000 passengers per day.

The first section has a length of 11.2km and serves ten communes with eighteen stations. Unlike most of the other new lines, the creation of line T7 was not an occasion to bring about a reduction in road traffic along its course and this required a great deal of new road construction. The RD7 had two traffic lanes for each direction, as it still does, but these now encompass a double-track tramway and there is also a parking lane and a cycle track on each side. New pavements, each 5m wide, were laid down. All this required a widening of the road surface from 20m to 40m, carried out while still maintaining existing traffic levels, and in turn this required the demolition of some property and the felling of a large number of trees, which have since been replaced by a larger number of pines and oaks. At several junctions, road underpasses have been closed. Two bridges have been built to take the line over the junctions with roads A86 and A106.

Most of the first part of the line is built on reservation on the RD7, but there are three deviations

from that. As these involve several right-angle bends, the average speed over this section is reduced. The first serves the interchange with the TVM busway and other bus services at Porte de Thiais. The second leaves the main road at the commercial centre of la Belle Épine, a centre with 2,800 employees, linked to the tram station by a pedestrian footbridge. The line here also serves the centre of the Commune of Rungis and some residential areas before reaching Rungis-la Fraternelle station on RER line C. The third deviation serves the new centre known as Coeur d'Orly, a centre of hotels, congress centres and boutiques. It then goes on to serve the airport's freight terminals and passes under the service area to Orly-Sud, where there is a link via the Orlyval line into the airport. Having rejoined the RD7, it then runs on to its present terminus in the commercial centre of Athis-Mons.

Rolling Stock

Line T7 has yet another variant of the Alstom Citadis design of tram, a new version of the Citadis 302, of which 19 have been delivered for this first section as part of a combined order for trams for lines T7 and T8. These will be followed by a further twelve when the extension to Juvisy is opened. The trams are double-ended and there are five modules per car. Regenerative braking is fitted. Lighting is by LED and for the first time in a Paris tram, there are information screens in the saloons, giving details of the next stop, the next principal stops and connexions with other lines. The interior and exterior of the trams were designed by the firm of MBD Design and they are rather different to earlier deliveries of this type, having a larger windscreen, intended to give a more welcoming appearance. The total cost of the rolling stock was €53 million, this being financed by STIF, and in recognition of this, the livery is silver grey and white on the roof and below the windows, which have a black surround, and a band of RATP green above. Internally the prevailing colour scheme is blue, commemorating the time when the N7 road was the principal highway leading to the Mediterranean. The external livery was the work of the agency Pixelis, while the internal scheme was created in Alstom's design office.

Technical details

Length 32.7m, width 2.40m, 4 x 120kW motors, 200 passengers, 54 seated.

Depot and workshops

As the line is not connected to any other tramway or métro line, it was necessary to give it its own workshops. The depot is located directly off the running line at Vitry-sur-Seine, on the site of a former car scrap yard. Construction began early in 2011. There are two buildings, the principal housing the maintenance centre, the running depot and the washing facilities. The technical centre is located in the second and smaller building and there are open-air sidings for 31 trams, although these will in future be partially covered by a new housing development. Great emphasis has been placed on the qualities of the depot, both as a building which benefits the environment of the area and which respects the general environment in its use of water and electricity. Insulation of the buildings has been carefully studied and there is a maximum use of natural light. Hot water is furnished by solar panels. The complex occupies an area of 24,900 square metres.

The public enquiry for the extension to Juvisy was held from 21 May to 22 June 2013 and the DUP was issued in November. It will be 3.7km long, with six stations, and will be traversed in ten minutes. It will serve the centre of Orly-Rungis, the second largest centre of employment in Île-de-France, and should open in 2018. The cost of the infrastructure is estimated at €198 million, to which has to be added €33 million for twelve additional trams, this being met by STIF.

Reference

Ville rail &Transports 4 June 2013.

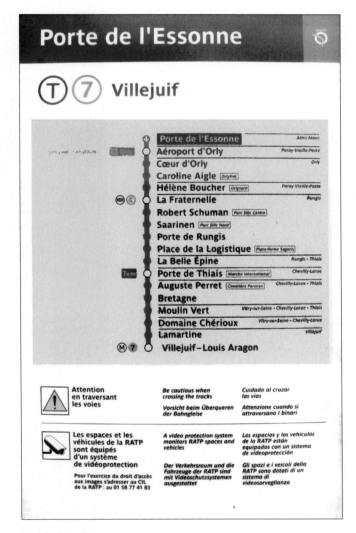

9.1. The line diagram

9.2 Villejuif Louis Aragon Métro station lies underneath a rather awful example of the architecture of the 1970s, in the shape of a multi-storey car park, which also houses the Métro station and facilities for RATP staff. Looking north, the bus station is on the right and the tram station on the left. This view of the works on the latter, taken on 5 May 2013, shows the layout.

9.3. The works were not confined to the west side of the complex but spilled over into streets on the east side, forcing buses to make awkward diversions to reach the bus station. Renault Agora no.3301 negotiates one of the work sites on 29 June 2012, while working on line 286 to Antony RER station.

9.4. The station in service, 11 July 2014.

9.5. A large sign on the wall of the station offices reassures passengers that this is indeed the station for line T7.

9.6. The station then known as Centre Commercial de Villejuif, under construction on 5 May 2013, looking towards the terminus.

9.7. In the event, the station opened with the more poetic designation of Lamartine. No.717 stops on a southbound working on 18 March 2015.

9.8. Works at the future station of Moulin Vert on 6 May 2013.

9.9. The station in service on 11 July 2014. No.710 is inbound to Villejuif.

9.10. A poster for the new depot,
6 May 2013.

9.11/9.12. The depot under construction on
the same date and in service on 11 July 2014.

9.12.

9.13. Work at the future station, Auguste Perret on 6 May 2013 .

9.14. Auguste Perret station in service on 18 March 2015. No.714 approaches.

9.15. No.713 approaches Porte de Thiais on 18 March 2015. This view gives an idea of the surroundings of line T7.

9.16. No.703 leaving the station which serves the commercial centre of la Belle Épine on 11 July 2014. Although the amount of space in the multi-storey car park offers competition to the trams, these are nonetheless very busy with shoppers at times such as Saturday afternoons.

9.17. As might be deduced from its name, Place de la Logistique serves only an industrial area and generally sees few passengers. No.707 slows for the curve into the station, 18 March 2015.

9.18. The elegant lines of the new generation of Citadis 302 trams are shown off on 11 July 2014 by no.712, approaching la Fraternelle after passing under the tracks of RER line C. While the surrounding area is unlikely ever to be classified as one of outstanding natural beauty, the amount of greenery has substantially increased in recent years, thanks to the tram line and to developments such as the office block on the left.

9.19. Just south of the latter station, the line turns sharply eastwards onto a fine piece of reserved track which allows the trams to display their potential for high speed. To ensure that motorists do not stray onto this private track, barriers are fitted and that for inbound trams is here being opened by the driver of no.706. If any car driver dares to dodge the barriers, he will find him/herself firmly stuck in a car trap, as marked by red and white diagonal stripes. 19 September 2015.

9.20. On the same date, airline passengers prepare to board no.712 at the station which serves Orly Airport.

9.21. Some long-distance travellers prefer to board at the terminus, Porte de l'Essonne. In the rain of 11 July 2014, no.719 uplifts those inbound to Paris.

9.22. This station also offers the unusual spectacle of a Citadis tram and Concorde in close proximity.

9.23. As off-peak and week-end services were at first rather infrequent, this early publicity was not quite accurate. However, such has been the demand for the trams that frequencies at these times have had to be increased, though still not quite to the level suggested here.

9.24. An interior view of one of the trams.

Chapter 10
Line T8 « Un Mode de Transport qui change nos Villes »

This line is more of a conventional street tramway and follows the course of line 54 of the first generation tramways for much of its length. It is often referred to as "Tram Y" from the form of its line diagram. It was initially mentioned in outline in the Schéma directeur of 1994 but was not seriously considered until 2005. It serves an area with a resident population of 77,000 and 12,000 students and was intended to facilitate suburb to suburb journeys and to be part of a large scheme of urban regeneration in Saint-Denis, favouring "les modes doux" (walking, cycling and public transport). It was intended especially to improve access to educational facilities. The DUP was issued on 11 February 2010 and work began later in that year. The "marche à blanc" began on 18 November 2014 and the line opened for traffic on 16 December 2014.

Line T8 is the first of the new tramways to incorporate a branch. It is in total 8.5km long and begins at Saint-Denis Porte de Paris station on Métro line 13, with a terminus on a large open space totally dominated by the viaduct of motorway A1 and its associated slip roads. From there it runs on street on the boulevard Marcel Sembat to Gare de Saint-Denis, where it crosses the tracks of line T1. The points to provide a single-line connexion for service purposes are in place on both this line and T1 but as of April 2015, the track between these had not been laid. The complex crossing was installed in the summer of 2011 and during that operation, service on that line had to be cut back. Line T8 goes on to serve a busy and densely populated commercial area with two more stations before dividing at Delaunay-Belleville into two branches, one to Villetaneuse and the other to Épinay. The former turns north and serves three stations before reaching its terminus at the Université de Paris Nord, whose 12,000 students provide much traffic for the service. There will be interchange at this point with Tram-Express-Nord when that opens in 2017. The other branch to Épinay has seven stations, the first of which serves an area of high-density housing dating from the 1970s. It also has interchange with line C of the RER and, in future, with the Tram-Express-Nord at Gare d'Épinay-sur-Seine, after which

it terminates at Épinay-Orgemont, another area with a dense population and one that is considered to have a number of social problems. Service operates at a frequency of three minutes on the common section at peak periods and five minutes at other times. The cost of the infrastructure, which was met by the Région, was €244.8 million (77.4%), the Département of Seine-Saint-Denis (19%), central government (2%), the Commune of la Plaine (1.5%) and the RATP (0.1%).

Rolling stock

Line T8 is worked by 20 Citadis 302 trams, nos.801-820, externally identical to those of line T7 and part of an order for 70 placed on 28 January 2011. The cost of these trams, €43 million, was met by STIF. This order took the total number of trams to the Citadis design over the 1,500 mark.

Depot and Workshops

These facilities are located at Villetaneuse Université on a short extension beyond the terminus and are in all respects similar to those provided for line T7.

References

Ville, rail &Transports, 9 February 2002, 13 November 2013, January 2015.

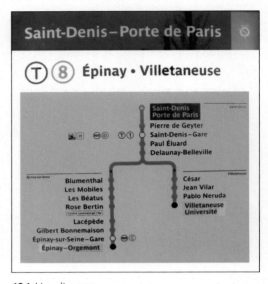

10.1. Line diagram.

10.2. In September 2013 a poster in the boulevard Marcel Sembat announces the arrival of the line.

10.3. Publicity for the new line at Porte de Paris Métro station promises that journeys on it will be swift, punctual and pleasant.

10.4. At Épinay terminus a hoarding gives details of the new service.

10.5. The terminus at Saint-Denis Porte de Paris affords easy interchange with a branch of Métro line 13. Having reversed, no.802 moves in to uplift passengers on the morning of 21 March 2015.

10.6. As far as the centre of Saint-Denis, line 8 uses an on-street reservation along the boulevard Marcel Sembat. No.813 runs on this section on 21 March 2015.

10.7/10.8. The first station is at place Pierre de Geyter. These views show the scene firstly on 26 September 2013 and secondly on 21 March 2015, with no.813 at the completed station.

10.9. The station of Gare de Saint-Denis is some distance from both the SNCF station and that of line T1. Nos.806 and 820 deal with the crowds on the morning of 21 March 2015, a day on which the level of pollution in Paris was such that, in an attempt to attract motorists out of their cars, all public transport was free for the entire day and, in the event, for the next two days.

10.10. Saint-Denis is the first place in Paris in which two tram lines (T1 and T8) cross each other and the points for a single-track connexion have been put in place on each line, but as of March 2015 these had not been connected.

10.11. Work in progress at the side of the Canal Saint-Denis on 3 May 2013.

10.12. Tall poles and heavy overhead mark the actual intersection of the two lines.

10.13 / 10.14. Works at la Poterie on 1 May 2013. A train of Corail Intercités heads towards the Gare du Nord. In the second view, work has been completed and no.805 heads for the suburbs.

10.15. No.816 takes the points for the branch to Villetaneuse, which leaves the main line west of this point.

10.16. The branch was opened for service before all the stations were completely furnished. An apology explains the situation at César, as no.811 calls on the same date.

10.17. On that Saturday afternoon, Villetaneuse terminus is quiet, but during the week it is always busy with some of the 12,000 students who attend the nearby university. The depot for line T8 is located beyond the station. No.811 awaits departure.

10.18. On the mainline, Rose Bertin station serves the large commercial centre, seen on the left. No.809 approaches.

10.19. No.809 approaching Gare d'Épinay. On the right, works are underway for the station of Tram-Express-Nord.

10.20. The station Gare d'Épinay, with no.804 uplifting passengers for Saint-Denis.

(Nos.14-20 were taken on 21 March 2015.)

10.21. Épinay gives a rather grey impression and the weather on this particular day certainly did nothing to lessen this. No.801 approaches the terminus.

10.22. An interior view of one of the trams, showing the slightly different colour scheme to those of line T7.

Chapter 11
Future lines

T9 Porte de Choisy – Orly-Ville

One of the busier lines of the first generation tramways was line 83, running in 1926 from Thiais and Choisy-le-Roi to Châtelet and carrying in that year over 11 million passengers. It had formerly been line 4 of the CGPT system. It was cut back to terminate at place d'Italie in January 1932, buses running from there to the city centre, and the remaining section was converted to motorbus operation on 30 October 1933. It was one of the two lines converted to trolleybus operation in the post-war period, in its case on 16 January 1950 and it then became line 183, worked by high-capacity Vétra VBF vehicles. Despite their success, the line was once again converted to motorbus operation on 1 April 1966. In 2012 it required a fleet of 38 of the latest MAN articulated vehicles. Much of the route is already on reserved busway, segregated from general traffic, but despite this and the modern bus fleet, the service is overcrowded for much of the day. There are delays due to traffic congestion and this leads to gaps in the service and bunching of buses. Over 57,000 passengers per day were carried in 2012 and, given the growth in the local economy, this figure may well increase in the near future.

The new tram line will run from Porte de Choisy to Choisy-le-Roi and the Fer à Cheval in Orly, a distance of 10.3km and will have 20 stations. For most of the route, it will run in an almost straight line along the road RD5, leaving this at the southern end to loop around the centre of Orly, where it will serve the cultural centre Louis Aragon. For the initial four kilometres it will use the existing busway and will therefore run in the centre of the road. From Vitry onwards, it will be on roadside reservation. Cycle lanes will be provided for much of the route and many pavements widened to improve pedestrian access. There will be interchange with tram line T3a at Porte de Choisy, with the future Métro line 15 at Vitry, with the Val de Marne busway at Rouget-de-Lisle and with RER line C at two stations in Orly. A passenger count of 70,000 per day is expected. Stations will be on average 650m apart.

The depot and maintenance centre will be located at les Voeux. There was some difficulty in the choice

11.1 Already much of the course of this line runs on central reservation. MAN articulated bus no.4623 negotiates a roundabout at Musée Mac Val on 29 June 2012. This museum is in fact the Museum of Modern Art, hence the curious structure apparently perched on the roof of the bus.

of site and this one is not ideal, as it will involve a crossing of the tracks of the Grande Ceinture. It was, on balance, the best option.

The probable cost of the infrastructure is given as €359 million – this being shared between central government (23%), the Région (54%) and the Département of Val-de-Marne (23%). The 22 trams required will cost €71 million and will be financed by STIF.

After a public enquiry which lasted from 2 June to 5 July 2014, the project was approved by STIF on 10 December and the DUP was issued on 2 February 2015. Work should begin in 2016, with completion in 2020.

T10 Antony – Clamart

In 2011 STIF began a study of a line to link the district of la Croix du Berny in Antony with Clamart, the general aim being to improve transport in Hauts-de-Seine. It has now been incorporated into the contract between central government and the Région covering the years 2015-2020. It will be 8.2km long, with 14

stations, and the expected cost is about €225 million at 2015 figures. The project is being undertaken by STIF, the Département of Hauts-de-Seine and the Région. Although there will be interchange with RER line B at Croix du Berny and with line T6 at Hôpital Béclère, there will be no direct interchange at its northern terminus, although Clamart station on the suburban line from Gare Montparnasse will be fairly near. The line may at a future date be extended northwards from its terminus in Clamart to meet line T2 at Issy-les-Moulineaux. The line colour will be lime green. The depot will be located at Châtenay-Malabry and the line will be worked by 14 trams, c40m in length.

References

Web site www.tramway-paris-orly-ville.fr

Der Stadtverkehr 10/2014. (New lines).

Chapter 12
Tram-trains

In recent years the greatest increase in commuter flows in Île de France has been concentrated on inter-suburban journeys. About half of all journeys are now made between suburban destinations, rather than to and from the centre of Paris. As the rail network is not structured to cater for these and as buses become snared in the increasing traffic jams, most people have preferred to use the private car for travel to and from work, thus creating even greater problems on the roads.

The Grande Ceinture (GC) railway line was first proposed under the Second Empire but, largely due to the outbreak of the Franco-Prussian war in 1870, little progress was made until President Mac Mahon signed the law authorising its construction on 4 July 1875. It was intended mainly to provide a bypass route for freight trains, but also with an eye to troop movements in the event of war, strategic considerations having grown in importance since the defeat of France in 1871. Of its total length of 121km, 91.5km plus a branch of strategic importance in the south and a duplicate line in the east, were of new construction. Existing tracks belonging to the various main line companies were used on a few sections. Like the Petite Ceinture, the line was worked by a syndicate of mainline companies. As built, it ran through open country, but much of the area it serves has been built up in recent years and is now densely populated. The first section to be used by the tramway, from Sartrouville to Noisy-le-Sec, was opened for traffic on 2 January 1882. Although passenger services ran over various parts of the line, it seldom carried a complete circular service and the trains which did run on it were generally infrequent and rather slow, taking, for example, almost four hours to travel from Juvisy to Noisy-le-Sec via Sartrouville. In the 1930s there were four trains each way per day on the section now being converted and these took just over an hour for the journey. It was essentially a line for freight and, despite increasing passenger numbers, the new SNCF, formed in 1938, wasted no time in ridding itself of the passenger services, the last passenger train on this section running on 15 May 1939.

In the post-war period much of the Ceinture was electrified. In the 1970s consideration was given to re-opening parts of the line to passenger traffic and

in 1969 the line between Orly and a new station at Pont de Rungis was reopened to passenger traffic; this service was extended to Massy-Palaiseau in 1977. Also, from 1984, TGV trains began to use parts of the Ceinture with "Interconnexion" services such as that from Lille to Lyon. In the early 1990s, a plan was developed to reopen the line between Sartrouville and Val-de-Fontenay to passengers, using existing tracks, but when it became apparent that the proposed frequency of a train every 15 minutes would seriously interfere with freight traffic and would cost FF1.6 milliard (€246 million), the plans were rejected. However, a passenger service on part of the western section of the line between Saint-Germain-en-Laye GC and Noisy-le-Roi via Saint-Nom-la-Bretèche began in December 2006. While this has been reasonably successful, it cost a good deal of money to bring the line and stations up to present-day standards for passenger trains and it has not attracted the expected number of passengers. That being so, thoughts of extending this kind of service over other parts of the Ceinture, as originally outlined in the plan Lutèce of the 1990s, were laid aside and instead, plans to run a service of tram-trains over three separate sections were formulated.

The first of these sections was originally known as the Tangentielle Nord (Northern Tangent) but in 2014 renamed Tram-Express-Nord. It will ultimately run from Sartrouville, on the main line out of Saint-Lazare and on Line A of the RER, via Argenteuil, Épinay and Villetaneuse to le Bourget and Noisy-le-Sec. The line runs on new track laid alongside the existing formation, but constructed to a reduced loading gauge. Gradients steeper than those of mainline railways, a trackbed width of 8.5m instead of 10m and curves of a tighter radius all combined to reduce the amount of land required for its construction, a clear advantage in built-up areas.

A preliminary study of the proposal was made in 1999 and the scheme was approved in principle in 2000, with this decision being followed by a more detailed study in 2003. As this gave a favourable report, a public enquiry was held in November/December 2006, also with favourable conclusions, and the DUP was issued on 27 May 2008 covering the section between Sartrouville and le Bourget.

Preliminary plans were adopted by the STIF in the summer of 2009 and the bulldozers began work at a site in Pierrefitte on 13 December 2010. The event was celebrated by a gathering of those involved with local politics and with transport and M Jean-Paul Huchon took advantage of the opportunity to remind those present that this was an historic occasion, the first stage in the realisation of a new form of transport between suburb and suburb. This sentiment was echoed by the President of Seine-Saint-Denis, who pointed out that this traffic flow had been for too long a neglected aspect of local transport and it was now time to make up the deficiency. Despite these encouraging words, the line had a singularly long gestation period, due to the very extensive works required to build a completely new railway line through a built-up area and adjacent to a very busy freight line. It was originally planned to open the 11km section from Épinay to le Bourget in 2014 but this schedule proved to be much too optimistic and the opening date was put back to July 2017, with a rider that a part of the line could be opened in 2016. All six level crossings along its length were closed, being replaced by bridges. Station platforms are long enough to permit the operation of two-car sets. An average speed of 50km/hr will vastly improve journey times with an end-to-end time of 35 minutes. At the western terminus of the first phase, there is interchange with line C of the RER and with tram line T8. Villetaneuse also provides interchange with line T8 and Pierrefitte with line T5 and line D of the RER. Line B and SNCF suburban services from Gare du Nord are met at le Bourget, line T1 at Drancy-Bobigny and also at Noisy-le-Sec, where there is also interchange with RER line E and in the future with new Métro line 15. Tram-trains will run every five minutes in peak periods and every 15 minutes at other times. It is hoped that this increase in connexions will result in a significant decrease in road traffic in the northern part of Île-de-France.

In the rebuilding of the stations, great care was taken to ensure that the new structures did not clash with the existing buildings, some of which are fine examples of the architecture of the former Chemin de fer du Nord. The station at Drancy, now a memorial to the thousands who were deported from it to the death camps in the second world war, has been carefully safeguarded. At various interchange stations the opportunity was taken to redecorate the buildings and improve facilities for all passengers.

Rolling stock

The line will initially be worked by 15 tram-trains of the Citadis Dualis design, part of the large order placed by SNCF in 2008, and when complete will have a fleet of 38 cars. In June 2014 STIF agreed to a firm order for the 15 cars at a cost of €88 million. The depot is located at Noisy-le-Sec.

Technical details

Length 41.97m, width 2.65m, 6 x 150kW motors, 251 passengers, 92 seated.

Tram-Express-Ouest

The second section to be converted will be the 25km between Achères Ville in the north-west and Saint-Cyr l'École in the south-west. As the line will be worked entirely under 25kV AC, it is unlikely that the tram-trains will proceed further into Versailles and passengers will have a rather inconvenient change if they wish to reach this important destination. This line will incorporate the section between Saint-Germain and Noisy-le-Roi mentioned above and platforms will have to be lowered in the re-opened stations to allow tram-train operation. A new link will be built in Saint-Germain to bring the tram-trains to Saint-Germain RER station but there is at present some discussion about the course this will take. This section will be opened first. The section between Noisy-le-Roi and Achères will be opened later. A headway of twenty minutes off-peak and ten minutes in peak periods is planned. The cost of the line will be between €230 million to €250 million, depending on the route chosen for the link in Saint-Germain. The DUP was issued in February 2014. The estimated costs, at 2011 figures, were €220 million for infrastructure and €43 million for rolling stock. It was stated that work could begin in 2016 for completion in 2018 but

this timetable now seems unlilkely. Apart from the terminals, interchange will be provided only at Saint-Nom-la-Bretèche, with the suburban services from Saint-Lazare. Funding for this line has not yet been agreed.

Tram-Express-Sud

This line of 20km will run from Massy-Palaiseau to Évry in the south-east of Île-de-France. It will run on the existing line of the Ceinture from Massy to Savigny-sur-Orge, then on a new section of railway line from Petit-Vaux to Épinay-sur-Orge and thence on new tramway-type infrastructure to Évry-Courcouronnes. Interchange with RER line B and, in future, with Métro line 18 will be available at Massy, with line C at Savigny-sur-Orge and with line D at the eastern terminus. There will be 16 stations. The estimated cost is €436 million plus €90 million for the rolling stock, both at 2015 prices. The line was approved by STIF in 2013 and the DUP was issued on 22 August of that year. It is hoped to open the line in 2019 but as yet no building work has started and, given the time-scale of Tram Express Nord, this date now seems unlikely. It is expected that it will ultimately carry 40,000 passengers per day. At a later date, possibly 2020, the 14.6km of the still-rural section of line, worked at present as part of line C, from Massy to Versailles Chantiers will be converted to tram-train operation. It is hoped that this will bring an additional 30,000 passengers per day. The estimated cost is €87.5 million. On both sections the tram-trains will replace trains of line C, thus simplifying the operation of that rather complex line. Some freight traffic will remain.

In October 2015 funding of €455 million was approved by STIF. Construction will begin in 2016.

References

To-day's Railways no.168, December 2009

Railway Gazette International, 16 December 2010.

Web site www.tangentiellenord.fr

12.1 and 2. Unfortunately it is not at present possible to obtain interesting photos of Tram-Express-Nord, but these two, taken at Épinay-sur-Seine on 21 March 2015 show that progress in being made.

Chapter 13
Preservation

Given the number and variety of trams which ran on the former system, it is unfortunate that only four survive and these owe their preservation to their being sold to other operators when the Paris system closed and were therefore available when the preservation movement began in the late 1950s.

The only preserved motor cars are nos.505 and 579, built for the CGPT in 1907 and used mainly on the line Ivry-Châtelet. Both were sold in 1936 for use on a works tramway at Hagondage (Moselle) and no.579 was kindly donated to the AMTUIR group by the owners of the line when it closed in 1964. When the opening of line T1 was imminent, no.579 was fully restored to running order, fitted with a pantograph and repainted into the livery of the CGPT, to allow it to work on the new line. Unfortunately technical differences between old and new made this impossible and it had to remain in the Saint-Mandé museum. No.505 went to the Brussels museum in 1964. Its only appearance in service to date was on Sunday 19 September 2010, when it was one of the star attractions at the memorable running day held in Brussels, under the auspices of the UITP and the patronage of HRH Prince Laurent. All day long it performed brilliantly between Woluwe and Tervuren, somewhat slow in acceleration but running steadily and coping uncomplainingly with the full and standing loads it carried on each trip. Such was the enthusiasm for it that it was at times hard to find even a standing place and enquiries to the conductor about gaining a foothold were met by a simple "Vous pouvez essayer" (You can but try).

Nos.505 and 579 are equal-wheel bogie cars with an off-centre entrance and separate saloons for passengers travelling in first and second class. Internally they resemble the earliest cars on the Métro, with much varnished wood. They were part of a series of 100 placed in service in 1907. These trams had an unladen weight of 19 tonnes.

The preserved trailer cars, nos.1535 of 1926 and 1630 of 1931, were both constructed by the STCRP. The latter was sold to the undertaking of Marseille in 1938 and ran there for rather longer than it had done in Paris. It was acquired by the museum group when the Marseille system closed in 1960. These are also centre-entrance cars and in both cities no.1630 worked as part of a "rame reversible", a reversible motor/trailer set. It is currently in the AMTUIR store at Chelles.

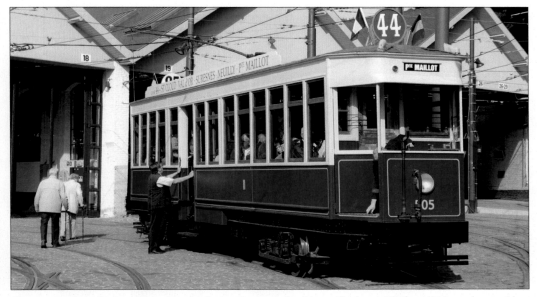

13.1. As soon as he finds whatever it is that he has dropped, the driver will take no.505 from Woluwe depot with another capacity load for Tervuren. The line number is correct for both Paris and Brussels; line 44 in the former ran in 1926 from Porte Maillot to Saint-Cloud and in the latter line 44 is still Montgomery-Tervuren.

13.2. When these passengers have alighted on the loop terminus there, the tram will immediately be stormed by another hopeful crowd. On the right, a PCC car from den Haag makes an interesting contrast.

13.3. An view of the second class saloon of no.505.

(nos. 1-3 were taken on the UITP running day in Brussels, 19 September 2010.)

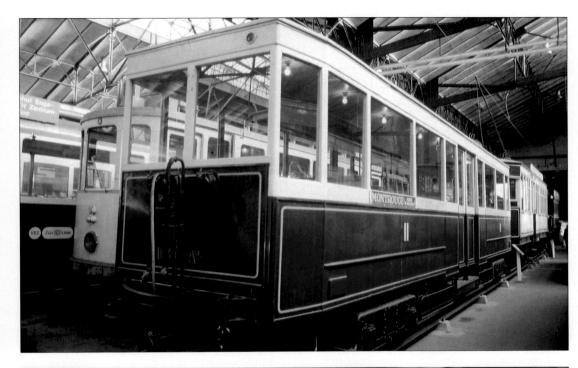

13.4. Trailer no.1629, in STCRP livery, in the former AMTUIR museum at Saint-Mandé. No.505, then numbered 579, stands in front.

13.5. In the absence of any other preserved cars some enthusiasts have collected early tin-plate models of Paris trams. The example seen here is of a two-axle double-decker of the Nogentais undertaking. The truck was quite definitely not of the Brill 21E type on which these cars ran. These models were shown in an exhibition held in the Technorama in Winterthur (CH) in June 1990.

Chapter 14
The Funiculars

Setting aside the Belleville line, which was a cable tramway, two funiculars have operated in Île-de-France, one of which still runs to-day, though not as a funicular.

1 Montmartre

A very small part of the transport system of the city may well be the best known to visitors – the Montmartre funicular.

The Butte (hill) of Montmartre lies just to the north of the inner wall of the city and from at least the 11th century became a venue for pilgrimages to the convent founded at that time and also for leisure, the two often being closely connected. Queen Marie de Médicis visited it in 1615, accompanied by about 60,000 citizens of Paris. The convent was closed down during the Revolution in 1794 and in the 19th century Montmartre became something of an industrial centre, with 30 mills in operation. A railway of some kind was built to serve the area, but nothing is known about it and it had disappeared by 1890. In 1873 work began on the extraordinary church known as the Basilique du Sacré Coeur (Basilica of the Sacred Heart), which was finally opened in 1891. A primitive funicular, with one wagon, was installed to take the materials up to the site and was dismantled when the building operations were completed. The church was intended to atone for the "sin" of the socialist Commune of 1871 and it soon attracted thousands of visitors. The area was also becoming a tourist attraction. As the flight of 222 steps leading up to the church proved to be something of an ordeal for many of these visitors, the City commissioned a report into the feasibility of building a funicular and as this was favourable, it was decided in 1899 to build a funicular from place Saint-Pierre to the rue Lamarck, adjacent to the church. To avoid having to seek approval from central government, the line was built on land already belonging to the City. It was built by the Société nouvelle des Établissments Decauville who were also the operators and, without waiting for the issue of a formal concession, they opened it to the public on 12 July 1900, just a week before the Métro and in time to cope with the large number of visitors who came to see the international exhibition. On 2 August 1901 a formal agreement with the City specified a concession that was to run for 30 years. The rental was to be 15% of the gross receipts. The line was operated by water power and the City supplied water at 30 centimes per ten cubic metres.

As built, the line was a double-track counterbalance funicular, 102.8m long. The difference in height between the stations was 37m, giving a ruling gradient of 36%. and a Strub rack rail laid between the running rails provided emergency braking, the service brake being worked by brakesmen who travelled on the cars. A speed of 1.5m per second was reached, giving a journey time of 70 seconds. The gradient was (and is) 350mm/m. The cars had stepped compartments and the platforms were arranged to correspond to these. They could carry 48 passengers each. Pre-1914 the fare was ten centimes for the ascent and five for the descent, but workmen were granted a special fare of five centimes in either direction – the funicular was not only for tourists. It proved to be very popular and carried about one million passengers annually.

The line was closed for modernisation in November 1931, soon after the concession had expired and the STCRP instituted a bus service, using Renault KX1 single-deckers, with driver-only operation. These were unpopular and passenger numbers slumped to about 250,000 per year. After some discussion, and given the unpopularity of the buses, the City decided in December 1933 to convert the funicular to electric traction, with new cars, and to hand over operation to the STCRP. The cars, which could accommodate 50 passengers, had a single compartment with a flat floor and stations were altered to match. The rack line was given up in favour of wheel-mounted brakes which could clamp the car to the rails if necessary. The line could now run at a speed of two metres/ second, but the overall time remained 70 seconds. The fare, in either direction, was now set at that of a one-stage bus ticket. Operation was resumed on 2 February 1935 and continued successfully for many years, under the auspices of the CMP from 1942 and the RATP from 1 January 1949. At an unknown date, but very probably at that time, the line was transferred to the control of the Métro, as a branch of line 2. The fare then became that of a standard single ticket of the rail system. In 1962 the line was briefly closed to allow upgrading of the electrical supply and at the same time new cabins were provided. These had aluminium bodies, rubber suspension and fluorescent lighting. A further improvement was the conversion to automatic operation in 1975, when the stations were modernised. The line was then carrying about 1.5 million passengers annually and there was a spectacular growth in passenger numbers between that year and 1989, when 2.35 million people used the line, about 80% of these being tourists. While formerly the majority of passengers had been carried in the up direction, the difficulties of parking coaches in Montmartre had led to an increased number of descending passengers and so to a better balance of traffic. There was, however, a good deal of congestion at peak tourist times and on the occasion of special services in the church. Despite this success, the funicular remained in deficit, receipts covering only 45% of expenses.

The RATP therefore decided on a complete modernisation of the operation and, having carried out a survey of passenger opinion among both tourists and local people, ended service on 30 September 1989. Complete modernisation was then carried out by the firms of Schindler and Akros, the former being responsible for the control system and the cables and the latter for the cabins. The stations were rebuilt in an airy, modern style, with much use of glass and stainless steel. The total cost was FF60 million (€9.23 million) and the line reopened on 4 October 1990.

The line is no longer a funicular but an inclined lift, operated by cabins that are totally independent of each other. At off-peak periods, service can be worked by a single cabin and it is no longer necessary to shut down the entire operation if work has to be carried out on one track. A detector on each platform notes the number of passengers as they arrive and, if no cabin is waiting, it sends a signal to bring one into service A similar detector within the cabin measures the weight of the passenger load and gives the starting signal when that figure has reached 80% of capacity. At quiet periods, the maximum waiting time is limited to five minutes, after which the cabin sets off, even if there are only a few passengers on board. Similar signals control braking and the opening and closing of the doors. Cable speed is now 3.5m/second and journey time is only 40 seconds. The cabins, designed by Roger Talon, can accommodate 60 passengers and as a result of these improvements, the line can now carry 2,000 passengers per direction per hour, double the former figure. The number of operating staff has been reduced to two, both based in the lower station, and all staff working on the line have, voluntarily, followed a course in English. Operation is now more flexible than formerly and congestion has decreased significantly, while off-peak service is provided much more economically.

The line now functions faultlessly in its modern form and carries 0.01% of the RATP's passengers, but the signs outside Abbesses Métro station and at the stations themselves still guide the tourists to the "funiculaire" and to Parisiens it is still "le funi".

2 Meudon Bellevue

Even in its lifetime, this line was much less well known.

The slopes above the banks of the Seine at Meudon were in the late 19th century a popular place for excursions from the city. Many of its citizens, on Sundays and holidays, took advantage of the boats which operated on the Seine to come down to Meudon for some fresh air and the chance to enjoy a meal and a drink in one of the small restaurants, perhaps with dancing afterwards. After 1889, some also came by train from Saint-Lazare or Invalides, alighting at the station known as Bellevue-Funiculaire. That line now forms the central part of line T2. However, the climb of 150m up from the quay or the station could be a trifle daunting.

In 1891 a company to build and operate a funicular was formed by two local businessmen, MM Paul Huette and Gabriel Thomas, the former being also a local councillor. The capital of the company was FF200,000. The line opened in 1893 and ran from the landing place of the river steamers up to the terrace of the Observatory, where horse-drawn carriages waited to take visitors further into the forest. It was 183.3m long, the difference in height was 52m and the gradient was 300mm/m. For its entire length, the line ran on a metal viaduct. It was single, with a passing place at the half way point. The cable was powered by a 60hp steam engine located in the lower station; a second engine was provided to cope with any breakdown of the first. Service braking was by hand but a Riggenbach rack rail afforded automatic emergency braking if the cable should break. The carriages, built by the Société Franco-Belge, had four compartments, arranged in steps, and could carry 52 passengers, 16 of these seated.

Fares were originally 10c up or down on weekdays, that for the ascent being doubled on Sundays and holidays. The line proved popular and in 1911 carried 311,602 passengers. Service was suspended in 1917 and not resumed until Easter 1922. The war and the arrival of the motor coach had changed leisure habits and fewer passengers now used the funicular. It was operated only from April to September, then from 1932 only on Sundays and holidays. By then it was carrying only 57,000 passengers per year and by 1934 this figure had decreased to 32,292. It was closed in 1935 and the company was dissolved in March 1938. The viaduct was destroyed in an air raid on 4 June 1942. In 2005 the RATP commissioned a study into the building of a funicular between Meudon station on line T2 and the SNCF station of Bellevue, on the line to Versailles. As nothing more was heard of this proposal, the outcome of the study must have been unfavourable.

Reference

Paris Métro Handbook. Brian Hardy. Capital Transport, Harrow. Second edition, 1993.

14.1. Looking up to the Sacré Coeur in the early days of the line. Did carriages pulled by goats offer a rival service or were the animals there to refresh visitors with milk?

14.2. The Montmartre funicular in service on 19 April 1968.

14.3. Saturday morning crowds at the lower station on 19 September 2015, when for a time only one car was in service and the tourists were becoming impatient.

14.4. A car of the present system near the upper terminus.

14.5. Despite the altered method of operation, the name, after twenty years, is unchanged.

14.6. The passing place on the Bellevue funicular, as depicted on a commercial card, posted in September 1927.

Abbreviations

AMTUIR	Association pour le Musée des Transports urbains, interurbains et ruraux	**PDU**	Plan des Déplacements urbains	**SYSTRA**	Système des Transports. (Title of SOFRETU after merger with SNCF subsidiary in 1995)
CFN	Compagnie des Chemins de fer Nogentais	**PS**	Parti Socialiste		
		RATP	Régie autonome des Transports Parisiens		
CGO	Compagnie générale des Omnibus	**RER**	Réseau Express Régional	**STIF**	Syndicat des Transports de l'Île de France
CGPT	Compagnie générale Parisienne des Tramways	**RFF**	Réseau ferré Français	**TPDS**	Cie des Tramways de Paris et du Département de la Seine
		SNCF	Société nationale des Chemins de fer Français		
CMP	Compagnie de Chemin de fer Métropolitain de Paris	**SOFRETU**	Société Française des Études et Réalisation des Transports urbains	**TFS**	Tramway Français Standard
DUP	Déclaratioin d'Utilité publique			**UMP**	Union pour un Mouvement populaire. (Right wing political party, now renamed Républicain)
GC	Grande Ceinture	**STCRP**	Société des Transports en Commun de la Région Parisienne		
PC	Petite Ceinture				

Bibliography

General

Le Patrimoine de la RATP. Éditions Flohic. No date, c1995

Métropolitain. L'autre dimension de la ville. Report of a seminar organised by the Bibliothèque historique de la Ville de Paris, 21 and 22 November 1986. Mairie de Paris. 1988

Les Expositions Universelles et les Transports. Musée des Transports, Saint-Mandé. 1989

Transports l'An 2001 en Île-de-France. Michel Chlastacz et Marc Lomazzi, La Vie du Rail, Paris. 1991

Through the Cities . The revolution in Light Rail. Michael Barry. Frankfort Press, Dublin. 1991

Les Tramways Parisiens. Jean Robert. 3rd edition, 1992

Les transports en région parisienne. Pierre Merlin. La documentation Française, Paris. 1997

Métrocité – Le Chemin de fer métropolitain à la conquête de Paris 1897-1945. Sheila Hallsted-Baumert ed. Paris musées. 1997

Les Cahiers de la Mémoire no.6. RATP. July 2001

Double-Deck Trams of the World. Brian Patton. Adam Gordon, Brora. 2002

Paris Tram. Clive Lamming. Parigramme, Paris. 2003

Le Train spécial, no.37. Jean Tricoire, ed. Publitrans, Betschdorf. 1/2004

Le tramway à Paris et en Île-de-France. Jean Tricoire. La vie du Rail, Paris, no date, c2007

Tramways. Revue Générale des Chemins de fer. Éditions Delville, Paris. No.170, March 2008

Die Zukunft der Städte. Harald A Jahn. Phoibos Verlag, Wien. 2010

Atlas du Tramway dans les Villes Françaises. François Laisney. Éditions Recherches, Paris. 2011

Les Omnibus au Temps des Chevaux. Clive Lamming. Éditions, Évreux. 2011 (Covers tramways 1855 >1910)

Transports et urbanisme en Île- de-France. Pierre Merlin. La documentation Française, Paris. 2012

Les Tramways Parisiens 1910-1938. Clive Lamming. Éditions Atlas, Évreux. 2012

Les Tramways Parisiens de 1992 à nos jours. Clive Lamming. Éditions Atlas, Évreux. 2012

Enquête globale des Transports. Direction régionale et Interdépartemental de l'Équipment et Aménagement de l'Île-de-France. 2014

Tram Atlas Frankreich. Christoph Groneck and Robert Schwandl. Robert Schwandl Verlag, Berlin. 2014

Web sites of RATP, STIF and Tram-Express-Nord.

Periodicals

Connaissance du Rail (until 2012)

Réseaux Urbains

Ville rail et Transports

Tramways and Urban Transit

To-day's Railways Europe

Strassenbahn Magazin

Der Stadtverkehr

The annual publication *TRAMS*, published in Alkmaar, Netherlands, by de Alk.

Video

Some excellent footage of first-generation Paris trams in service can be found in the following two DVD collections:-

Paris Transports Atmosphères. GS films, Gérard Scher. 2006

Paris rétro, Paris roule. Des années 1900 à nos jours. Média 9. www.decouvrir-le-monde.com

The present line T3 is covered in the DVD *Tram de Paris – il est là!* La Vie du Rail, Paris.